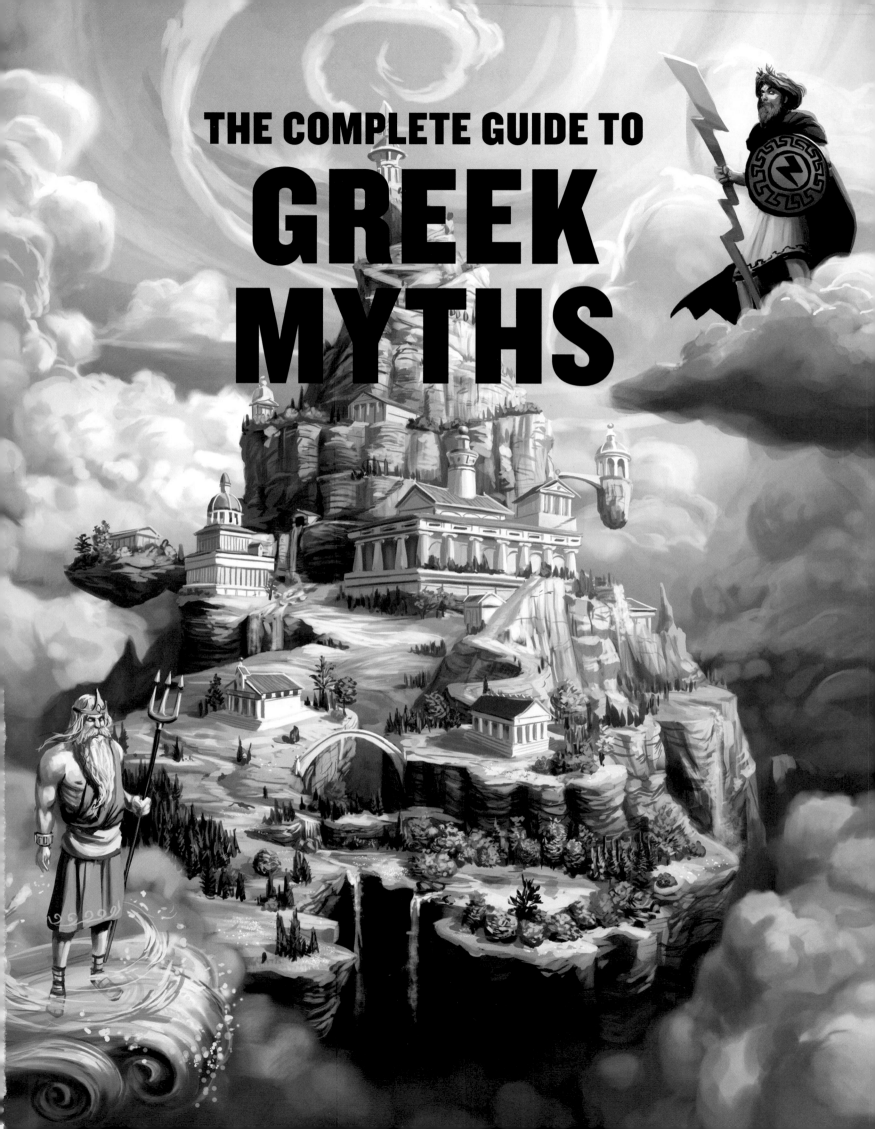

THE COMPLETE GUIDE TO
GREEK
MYTHS

An Imprint of Sterling Publishing
1166 Avenue of The Americas
New York, NY, 10036

ISBN: 978-1-4351-6162-7

Manufactured in China
Lot #:
2 4 6 8 10 9 7 5 3
11/15

Picture Credits

Shutterstock: Nazar Tosyfiv 4-5; Elena Schweitzer
51; HorenkO 2-144 (backgrounds).

Illustrations

Matthew Forsyth: 5bl, 108-109, 110-111,
112-113, 114-115, 116-117, 118-119, 120-121.
Leo Hartas: 4tr, 26-27, 30-31, 36-37, 52-53,
62-63, 74-75, 88-89, 90-91.
Jason Juta: 8-9, 10-11, 12-13, 22-23, 38-39, 49.
Gerald Kelley: 14-15, 80-81, 130-131, 132-133,
134-135, 136-137, 138-139, 140-141.
Mike Love: 16-17, 42-43, 54-55, 64-65, 76-77,
94-95, 96-97.
Tom McGrath: 1, 20-21, 40-41, 56-57, 66-67,
84-85.
Jani Orban: 2-3, 4bl, 5tr, 6-7, 28-29, 34-35,
46-47, 60-61, 68-69, 70-71, 72-73, 78-79, 82-83,
98-99, 100-101, 102-103, 104-105, 106-107, 122-
123, 124-125, 128-129.
Franco Rivoli: 18-19, 24-25, 32-33, 44-45, 58-59,
92-93, 126-127.
Amanda Sartor: 86-87.

THE COMPLETE GUIDE TO
GREEK MYTHS

HEATHER DAKOTA

Sandy Creek
NEW YORK

CONTENTS

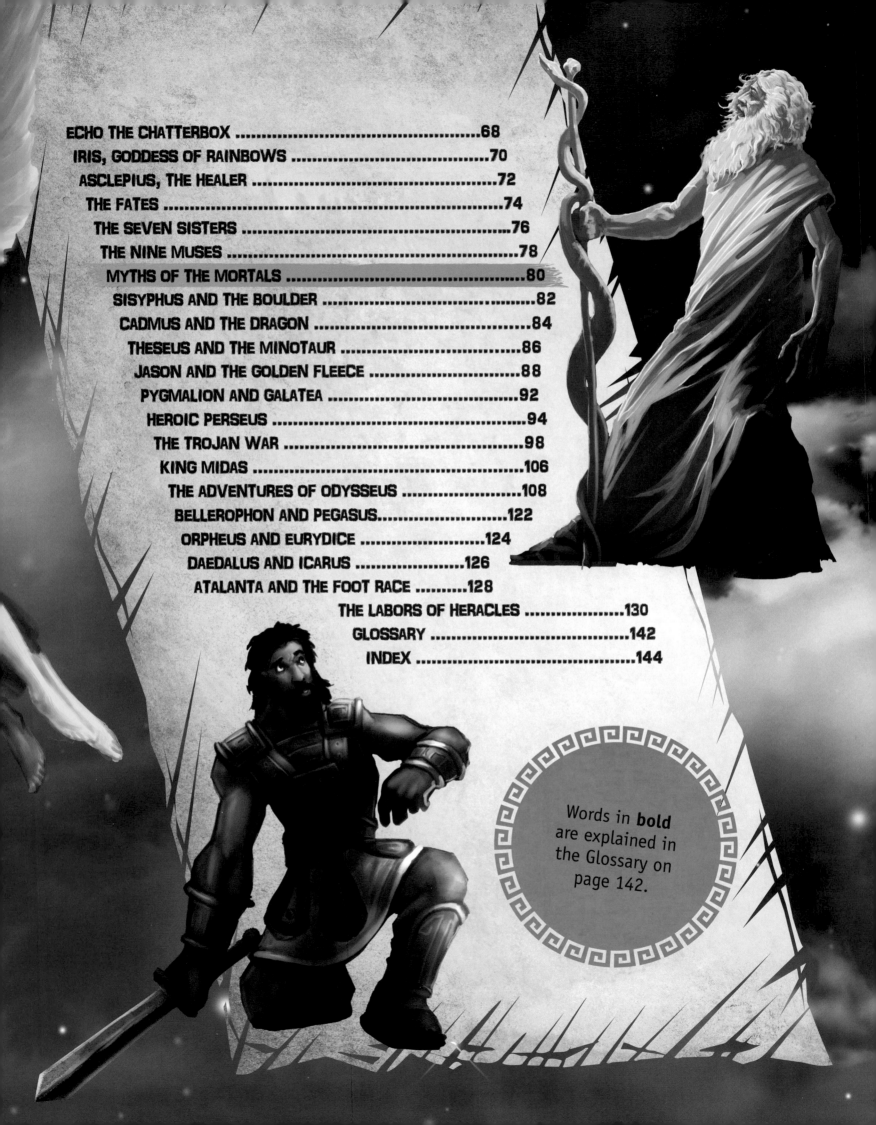

Words in **bold** are explained in the Glossary on page 142.

INTRODUCTION

The Ancient Greeks created myths and told stories to explain the world around them—the rising and setting of the Sun, the seasons, and the origins of the universe, people, and nature. The stories were also a way to show people how they should behave in times of peace and of war, and how to live in harmony with others.

Myths evolved as stories and were told over and over again, and passed from one generation to the next. The stories were first told around 900 BCE and were written down by great Greek writers, such as Homer, Aeschylus, and Hesiod. Myths have had a huge effect on history, culture, and life around the world. They shaped not just the ancient world, but also the modern world, as well as the language we speak. People who love themselves are *narcissistic*, a person's weakness is his or her *Achilles's heel*, and you've probably used an *atlas* to look at our world. All these words come from Greek myths, as you'll soon see.

Myths are filled with adventure, love, betrayal, war, jealousy, loyalty, tragedy, and heroic deeds. There are mighty gods and goddesses, noble heroes, and terrifying monsters to fuel the imagination.

Get ready to experience the richness and beauty of the gods, hold your breath with the heroes, and witness the power of these ancient myths.

MYTH AND REALITY
Some myths are based on characters and places that really existed, or events that really happened in the ancient world; others are entirely imagined.

MYTHS OF THE IMMORTALS

The whole universe, including its first beings, emerged from **Chaos**—a huge emptiness. Chaos came into being before creation, before even the elements existed, and ruled over confusion.

The first gods that came from Chaos were called the **Primordials**. They were astronomical in size, immortal, and had immense powers. They made up the very fabric of the Universe and—between them—forged the Earth.

The children of Chaos were Gaia (Earth), Tartarus (the Underworld), Eros (Desire), Nyx (Night), and Erebus (The Darkness of the Underworld). Some of the Primordials had children with other deities; some produced offspring on their own.

Gaia had two sons, Uranus (Sky) and Pontus (Water). Gaia created Uranus to be her equal and together the two had many children, including the mighty Titans and Giants—deities of great strength.

Two of the Titans, Cronus and Rhea, were to become the parents of Zeus (see page 23), who would later rule over the Gods on Mount Olympus, and become the key figure in countless Greek myths.

The primordials Uranus, Nyx, Gaia, and Pontus (clockwise from top left) create Earth.

MYTH AND REALITY

Almost every ancient culture has myths to explain the origins of the universe. Usually the universe emerges from nothing, or from chaos.

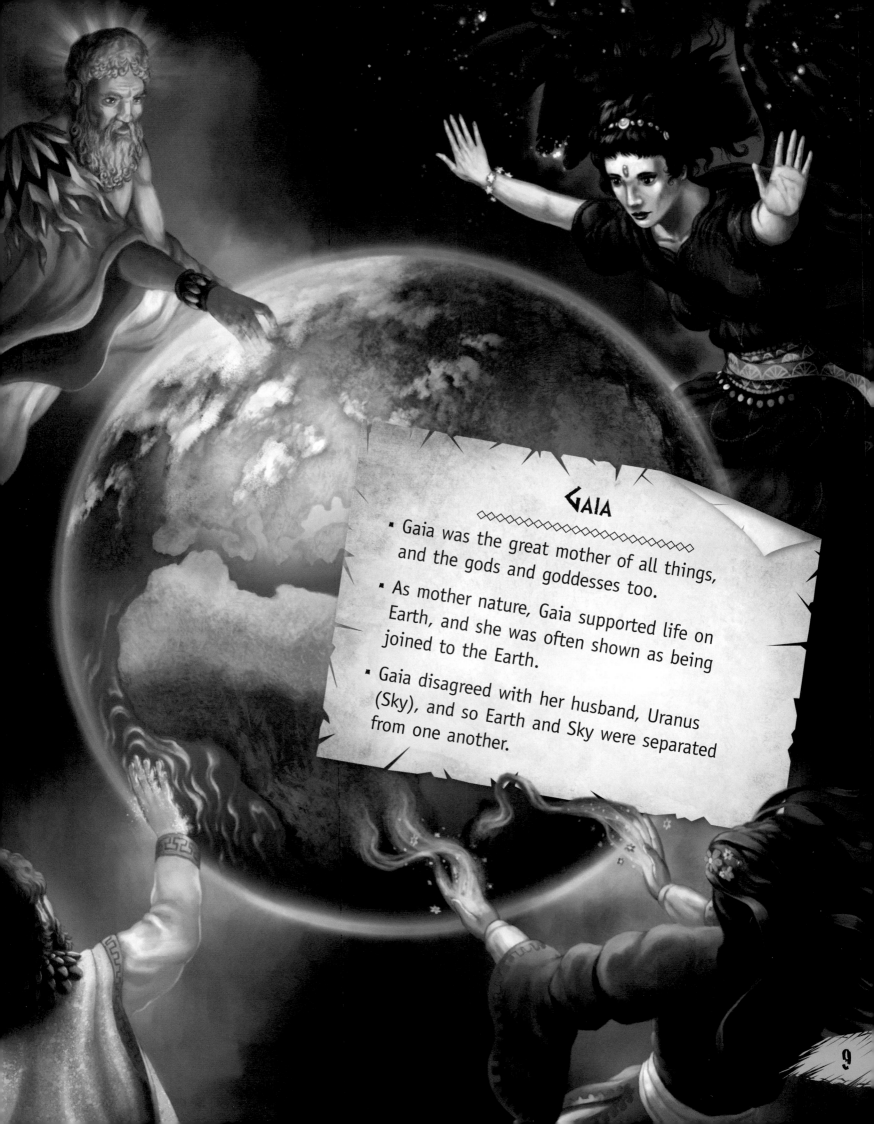

GAIA

- Gaia was the great mother of all things, and the gods and goddesses too.

- As mother nature, Gaia supported life on Earth, and she was often shown as being joined to the Earth.

- Gaia disagreed with her husband, Uranus (Sky), and so Earth and Sky were separated from one another.

NYX AND HYPNOS

Nyx (Night) emerged from Chaos at the beginning of the world. She was a beautiful goddess with large black wings. She lived in the Underworld during the day and came out into the world only at dusk. With Erebus, she gave birth to Aether (Atmosphere) and Hemera (Day). On her own, she gave birth to many other offspring, including Apate (Deceit), Geras (Old Age), Ceres (Doom), Momos (Blame), Hypnos (Sleep), and Thanatos (Death). Nyx appeared in some of the stories of the later gods and she was the only goddess feared by Zeus. One day,

Hera, the wife of Zeus, spoke to Nyx's son, Hypnos (Sleep). She persuaded him to make Zeus fall asleep, because she wanted to kill Heracles, one of Zeus's sons. While Zeus slept, Hera summoned up a great sea storm to try to kill Heracles, who was sailing to his home.

When Zeus woke up, he was furious and threatened to punish Hypnos by casting him into the Underworld. However, Hypnos quickly ran to his mother's side. Zeus was forced to take back his threat. There was no way he would cross the mighty Nyx.

MYTH AND REALITY
In myth, Hypnos (Sleep) had a twin brother named Thanatos (Death). For the Ancient Greeks, sleep and death seemed very similar.

Nyx protects her son Hypnos from the wrath of Zeus.

ii

Uranus represents air,
light, and energy,
while Gaia (below)
is the life-sustaining,
fertile Earth.

12

URANUS AND GAIA

Gaia, the Earth goddess, gave birth to Uranus, god of the sky. He lived in the mountains from where he looked lovingly down on his mother and sent her gentle rains that formed rivers and lakes. Gaia used these waters to make Earth fertile and produce trees, flowers, fruits, and grasses.

Uranus and Gaia had many children together. These included the twelve **Titans**, the **Cyclopes**—who were violent, one-eyed creatures—and the **Hecatoncheires**, who were mighty giants with 50 heads and 100 arms.

Uranus feared the great power of his children and came to hate them. He imprisoned them deep in the body of Earth, which caused Gaia great pain. Gaia became very angry and implored the Titans to overthrow Uranus. Led by the Titan Cronus, they rebelled against their father and fought him with a diamond **sickle** that Gaia had given them.

When the blood of Uranus fell into the sea, it created the goddess Aphrodite, as well as the **Giants** and the **Fates**.

MYTH AND REALITY
The idea of "Gaia"—the Earth as a planet that heals and controls itself—has been used by some modern scientists.

THE POWERFUL TITANS

The Titans were powerful and immortal gods. They ruled from the top of their stronghold, Mount Othrys, where they sat on their thrones.

The first generation of twelve Titans were all the children of Gaia and Uranus. There were six males, Oceanus, Hyperion, Coeus, Cronus, Crius, and Iapetus; and six females, Mnemosyne, Tethys, Theia, Phoebe, Rhea, and Themis. The Titans were responsible for different realms—for example, Oceanus was god of water; and Mnemosyne was goddess of memory.

Soon these Titans began to have their own offspring. Oceanus and Tethys gave birth to Clymene, Dione, Eurynome, Metis, and Styx. In turn Clymene and Iapetus had four sons, Epimetheus, Prometheus, Menoetius, and Atlas.

Each of the Titans had their own myths and stories: Atlas, for example, was the god of astronomy and navigation. He is best known for his punishment for fighting against Zeus—which was to carry the world on his shoulders for all eternity.

ATLAS

- Atlas was part of the second generation of Titans. He was the son of Iapetus, the god of craftsmanship.

- He lived in the far west of the world with his daughters, the Hesperides, goddesses of the evening and of sunset.

- Atlas gave his name to a mighty range of mountains in North Africa.

Atlas carrying the world on his shoulders.

MYTH AND REALITY
The word "Titan" has come to mean vast and powerful. The ship *Titanic* was the biggest movable object in the world when it was built in 1911.

ZEUS AGAINST CRONUS

Cronus was the youngest son of Uranus and Gaia. He was the leader of the Titans, and soon became drunk on power.

Long ago, Cronus's mother, Gaia, had warned him that one of his children would rise up and overthrow him, just as Cronus

had overthrown his own father, Uranus. So to protect his throne, Cronus devoured each one of his children just after they were born. His wife, Rhea, was distraught at the loss of all her children.

When her next son was born, she hid the baby in a cave, where he was raised by a

she-goat named Amalthea. Rhea gave Cronus a rock, wrapped in swaddling clothes, instead of her child. Cronus ate the rock, thinking it was his child.

The child—whose name was Zeus—survived and grew into an adult. When he was grown up, he returned to the court of Cronus and worked for his father as a servant. Here he gave Cronus a potion that made him vomit up all of his swallowed sons and daughters.

With his brothers and sisters freed from the belly of Cronus, Zeus led them in a rebellion against the Titans. He recruited the fearsome Hecatoncheires and the Cyclopes (see page 13) to fight on his side, and won the support of some of the Titans, including Styx, Prometheus, and Epimetheus. Fighting on the other side with Cronus were the rest of the Titans.

In the great battle that followed, Zeus and his army rained down thunder, lightning bolts, rocks, and flames on the Titans. After ten years of bitter war the Titans were defeated.

MYTH AND REALITY
Cronus was worshiped by ancient people as a god of agriculture. He was sometimes shown in art as an old man holding a sickle.

The elder gods, or Titans, are defeated by the Olympians.

17

THE END OF THE TITANS

After the war against Zeus, the defeated Titans were imprisoned in **Tartarus**—the deepest and darkest place in the Underworld, said to be as far from the surface of Earth as the surface was away from the heavens. Here they were guarded by the fearsome Hecatoncheires. Prometheus, who had fought alongside Zeus, was allowed to remain with the new ruling gods, while Atlas, who had fought against Zeus, was condemned to carry the world on his shoulders (see page 14).

Zeus and his brothers and sisters took their place as divine rulers on Mount Olympus. Many years later, Zeus forgave the Titans for fighting against him. He released them from Tartarus and made Cronus king of the **Elysian** Islands, home of the blessed dead.

THE HECATONCHEIRES

- The Hecatoncheires were three giants, each with 100 arms. Their names were Briareos, Kottus, and Gyges.

- They were the sons of Uranus, who thought they were so hideous that he threw them into Tartarus after their birth.

- Whenever they made an appearance, Earth shook and waves crashed on the land.

Cronus is chained in Tartarus, where he is guarded by the Hecatoncheires.

MYTH AND REALITY
According to Greek writer Hesiod, Tartarus was made when a giant bronze **anvil** fell from the heavens and made a deep hole in the Earth.

19

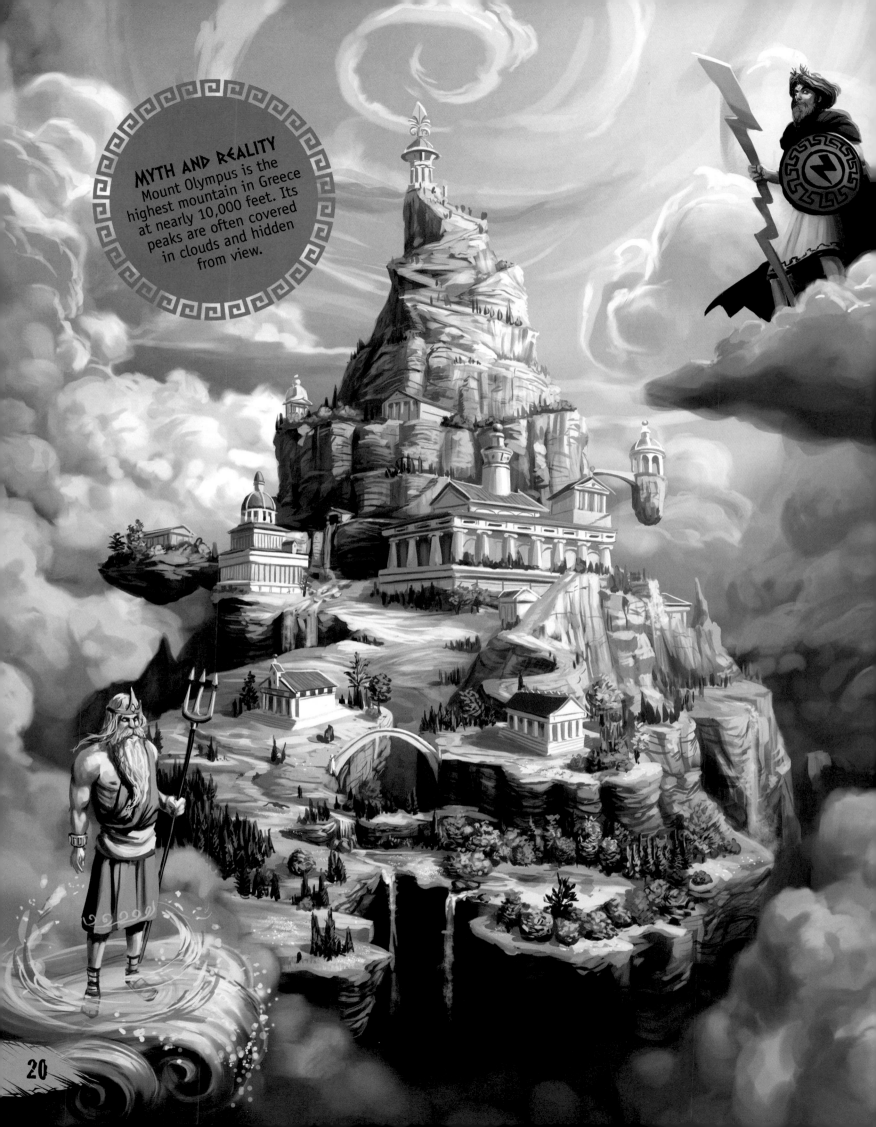

MYTH AND REALITY
Mount Olympus is the highest mountain in Greece at nearly 10,000 feet. Its peaks are often covered in clouds and hidden from view.

THE OLYMPIANS

Twelve gods lived on Mount Olympus after the defeat of the Titans. These gods—children of Cronus—were called the **Olympians**.

The three most powerful Olympians—Zeus, Poseidon, and Hades—drew straws to decide which of them would rule which parts of the universe. Zeus became the god of the sky, thunder, and lightning. His mighty weapons were the thunderbolt and his Aegis (shield).

Zeus was voted the supreme ruler of Mount Olympus, and also given the task of punishing other gods if they dared to lie, cheat, or otherwise misbehave. Poseidon became god of the sea, while Hades ruled over the **Underworld**. Hades did not live with the other gods on Mount Olympus. He preferred living alone in the Underworld.

◄- - - - | Zeus (top) and Poseidon (bottom) rule over the sky and the sea.

Zeus's wife, Hera—queen of the gods—lived on Olympus, along with her sisters, Demeter and Hestia, the goddesses of fertility and of the household. Hera was constantly jealous of Zeus's many love affairs with other gods and mortals.

The other gods on Mount Olympus were the children of Zeus. Ares, the god of war, was hated by both his parents, Zeus and Hera. Apollo and his sister Artemis ruled over music and fertility, respectively. Athena was the daughter of Zeus, and emerged directly from her father's forehead. Hermes was the messenger god who guided souls to the Underworld and carried messages from the gods on Olympus to mortals on Earth.

The last of the Olympian gods was Hephaestus, who was the god of blacksmiths, the **forge**, sculptors, and craftsmen.

ZEUS AND THE MORTALS

Zeus was considered to be the father of humans. He created them in his likeness and gave them a place to live on Earth. At first, in the so-called Golden Age, mortals lived among the gods. There was no grief, sorrow, or hard work. People were ageless beings who enjoyed feasts and **festivals**. They died peacefully after living long lives. Mortals were beyond the reach of evil and were provided for by the gods and goddesses. There was abundant fruit and livestock on Earth, so they lived in peace and harmony with one another, worshipping the gods and goddesses.

During the Silver Age, mortals had worse lives. They lived for a hundred years as simple, childlike beings, and then had short and sorrowful adult lives. They had to grow their own food and make their own shelters. They refused to serve the immortals or offer sacrifices to them. Zeus was so angered by this disrespect that he sent these mortals to the Underworld.

In the Bronze Age, Zeus created people who were tall, ferocious, and loved battle. All their weapons and armor were made from bronze, but their love of war meant that they all perished.

Then followed the Age of Heroes, when mortals performed heroic deeds. This was the time of Jason, Odysseus, and Heracles. The men and women of these ages faced loneliness and misery. Zeus allowed this suffering in order to teach mortals to worship the gods.

Finally came the Age of Iron—a time of great trouble, evil, dishonor, scorn, and violence. According to the Greek myths, we continue to live in the Age of Iron to this day.

Zeus had little regard for most mortals but he was always fair. He believed that humans created their own problems, which should not be blamed on the gods.

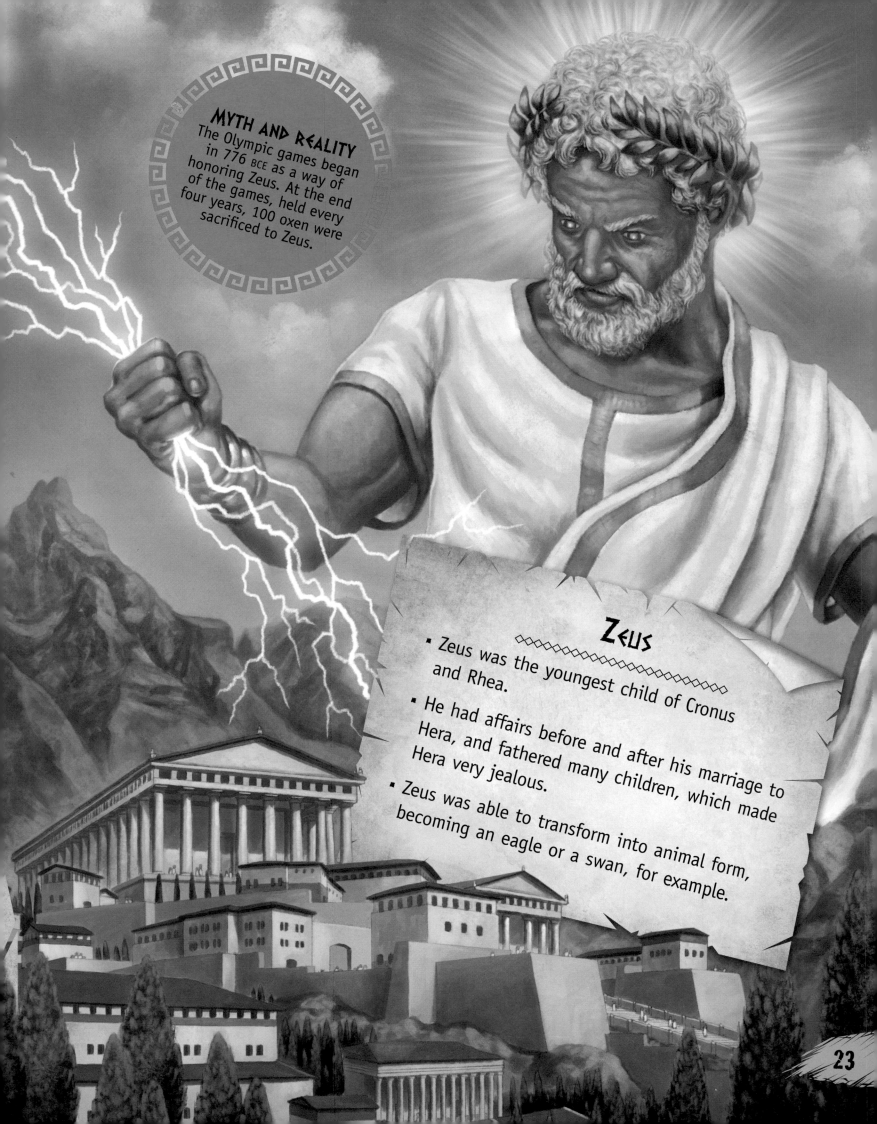

ZEUS

- Zeus was the youngest child of Cronus and Rhea.

- He had affairs before and after his marriage to Hera, and fathered many children, which made Hera very jealous.

- Zeus was able to transform into animal form, becoming an eagle or a swan, for example.

ZEUS BATTLES TYPHON

The goddess Gaia (see page 13) wanted to take revenge on Zeus for defeating and imprisoning her offspring, the Titans. She told her last son, the dreadful Typhon, to destroy Zeus.

Typhon was a huge monster with a snake's tail, a hundred dragon heads with fiery eyes, dark tongues, and a voice like thunder. He could whip up strong winds and throw fire from his mouth. His favorite weapons were red-hot rocks, which he flung at his enemies.

Typhon attacked Olympus, the home of the gods, spewing fire. Many of the gods fled in terror, but Zeus fought back, throwing thunderbolts at the monster. But Typhon was too strong. He grabbed Zeus and tore out his muscles and tendons—the parts

Typhon was the most
powerful of all the
monsters in Greek
mythology.

that attach the muscles to bones. He threw them away, leaving Zeus lying helpless on the ground.

Zeus called out in pain. Hermes—Zeus's son—heard his cries and came to the rescue. He found the pieces that Typhon had removed from Zeus's body, and sewed them back into his limbs. Then, Zeus attacked Typhon with renewed strength and chased him across the seas to the island of Sicily.

Finally, Zeus picked up Mount Etna—a huge volcano—and trapped Typhon beneath it. Typhon, being immortal, did not die. To this day, you can still see his fiery breath billowing from Mount Etna.

Pieces of Typhon's body torn off by Zeus's thunderbolts grew into other monsters, such as the Chimera (see page 123).

BIRTH OF ATHENA

Zeus really liked Metis and wanted to make her his wife. Metis was a Titan—one of the ancient gods who ruled before the gods on Olympus—and one of the wisest of them all. She didn't want to be with Zeus and tried to escape his attention by changing her form many times into various creatures, such as a hawk, fish, and serpent. Zeus was very determined and changed his form, too. He continued to pursue her until she gave up and became his first wife.

Before long, Metis became pregnant. An **oracle**—someone who could see the future—told Metis that she would have a girl. However, the Oracle also told her that her second child would be a boy who would overthrow Zeus. When Metis told Zeus about this prophecy, he became very angry and screamed at the top of his lungs. It was said that the scream could be heard all over the world.

MYTH AND REALITY

In ancient times, the people of Athens honored Athena every June in a great festival called Panathenaia. There were races, games, music, singing, and dancing.

ATHENA

- Athena was the goddess of war—a more thoughtful female version of Ares. She only fought in wars to defend her home.

- She was known for her bravery, wisdom, compassion, and love of the arts and crafts.

- The Parthenon—a huge temple in Athens—was dedicated to Athena. It is still one of the world's most amazing buildings.

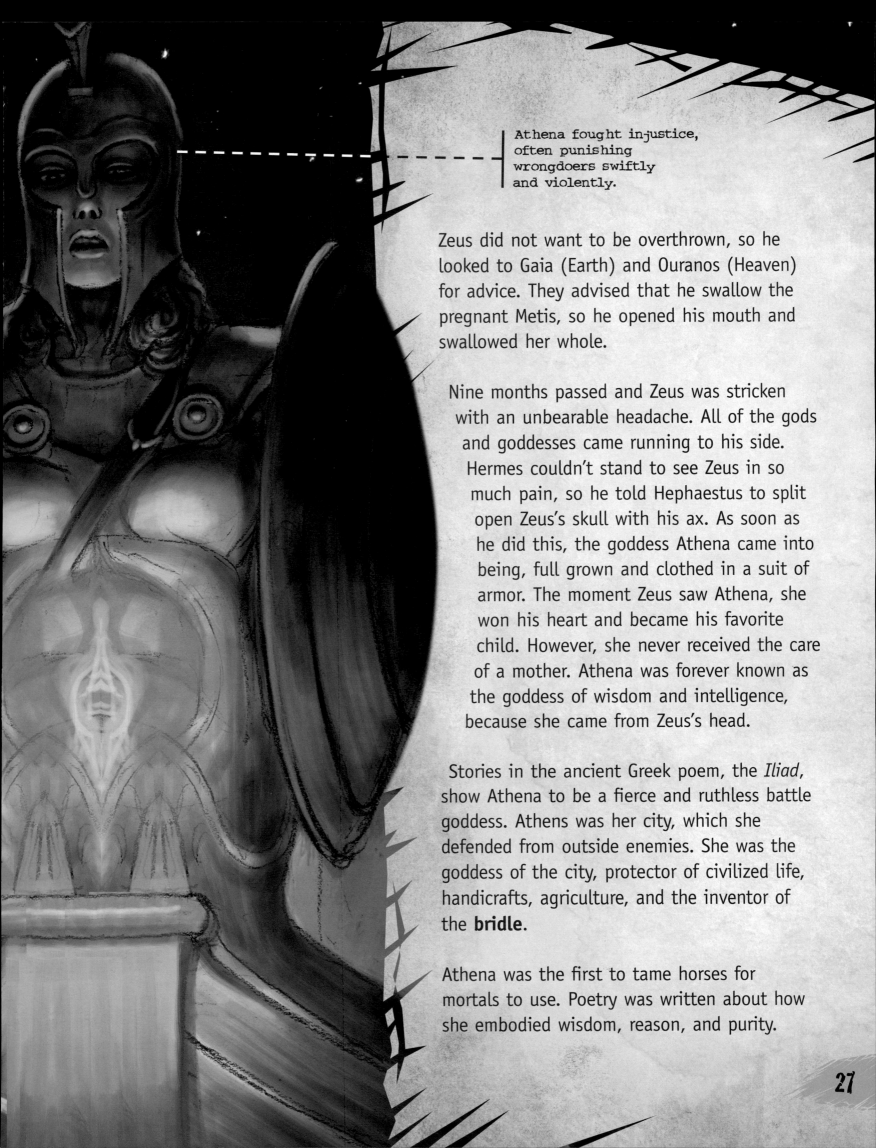

Athena fought injustice, often punishing wrongdoers swiftly and violently.

Zeus did not want to be overthrown, so he looked to Gaia (Earth) and Ouranos (Heaven) for advice. They advised that he swallow the pregnant Metis, so he opened his mouth and swallowed her whole.

Nine months passed and Zeus was stricken with an unbearable headache. All of the gods and goddesses came running to his side. Hermes couldn't stand to see Zeus in so much pain, so he told Hephaestus to split open Zeus's skull with his ax. As soon as he did this, the goddess Athena came into being, full grown and clothed in a suit of armor. The moment Zeus saw Athena, she won his heart and became his favorite child. However, she never received the care of a mother. Athena was forever known as the goddess of wisdom and intelligence, because she came from Zeus's head.

Stories in the ancient Greek poem, the *Iliad*, show Athena to be a fierce and ruthless battle goddess. Athens was her city, which she defended from outside enemies. She was the goddess of the city, protector of civilized life, handicrafts, agriculture, and the inventor of the **bridle**.

Athena was the first to tame horses for mortals to use. Poetry was written about how she embodied wisdom, reason, and purity.

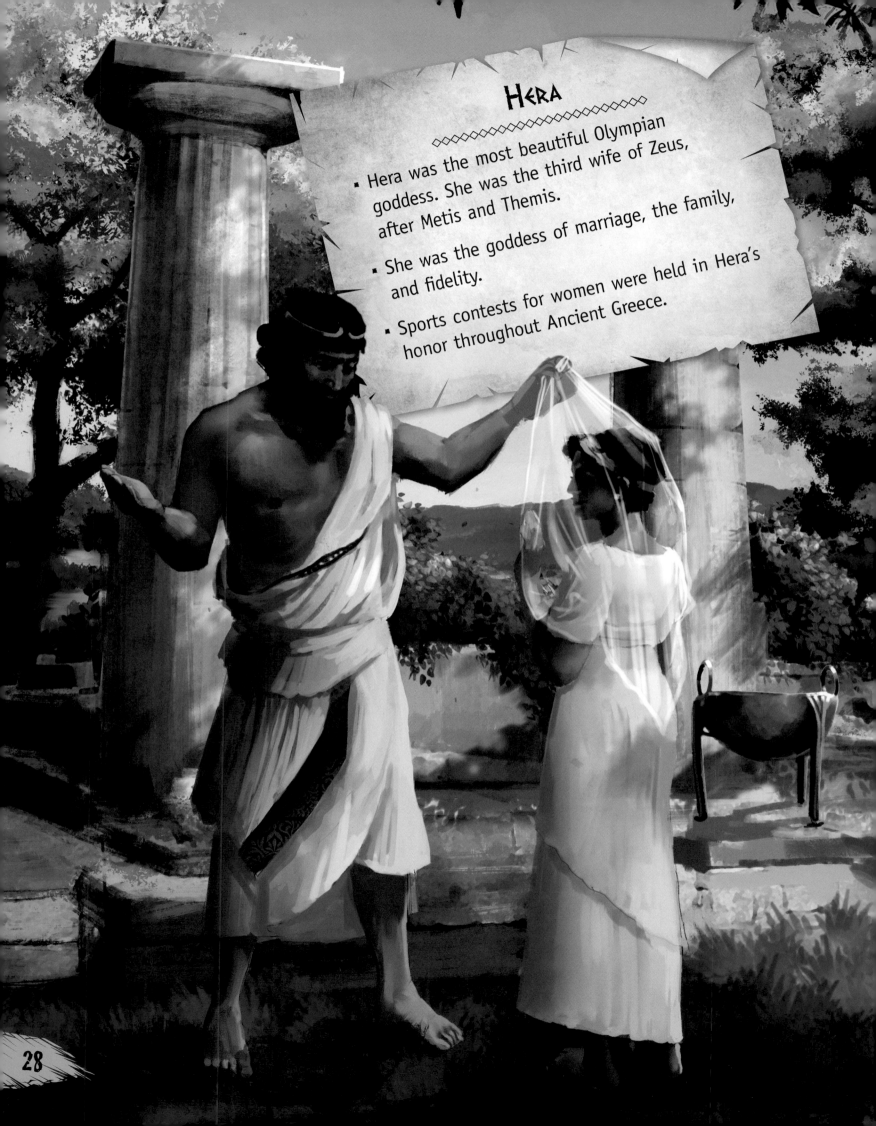

HERA

- Hera was the most beautiful Olympian goddess. She was the third wife of Zeus, after Metis and Themis.

- She was the goddess of marriage, the family, and fidelity.

- Sports contests for women were held in Hera's honor throughout Ancient Greece.

ZEUS AND HERA'S WEDDING

Zeus fell in love with the most beautiful of the goddesses—Hera. He wanted her as his wife because she was the only one who could match him in knowledge and power.

To seduce Hera, Zeus first turned himself into a cuckoo, then summoned up a bitter rainstorm. The cold rain fell, making the cuckoo wet and bedraggled. Hera saw the bird and felt sorry for it. She picked up the rain-soaked cuckoo and put it inside her clothes to keep it warm and dry. Zeus then changed back into a god and Hera agreed to become his wife.

They were married in the blissful Garden of Hesperides, on the western edge of the world. All of the gods and goddesses came to the wedding and brought gifts. Gaia, the goddess of the Earth, made a tree produce golden apples to honor the couple. Even Hades came from the Underworld for the ceremony. Their honeymoon lasted 300 years!

Hera became the goddess of marriage, protecting wives from their husbands, and punishing adulterers. Zeus had many love affairs and Hera became a jealous wife. It was said that the fights between Zeus and Hera were so bad that they shook Mount Olympus.

MYTH AND REALITY

Hera was worshiped widely in the Greek world. There were temples dedicated to her at Olympia, Argos, and on the island of Samos, where she was born.

ZEUS, HERA, AND IO

One day, when Zeus was sitting on his throne high on Mount Olympus, he spotted a bright reflection from the river Ianchus in Argos, Greece. Next to the bright light he saw a beautiful water **nymph** named Io.

Io was a priestess at the temple of Hera—the wife of Zeus. Enchanted by Io, Zeus descended from Olympus to meet her, and the two fell in love. Zeus knew that Hera would be very jealous, so he covered the world with clouds to prevent Hera seeing him with Io. Hera was no fool and soon became suspicious. She came down from Olympus to find out what was going on. To protect Io from Hera's anger, Zeus changed her into a white cow.

Hera commands Argus to keep Io away from her husband, Zeus.

Hera soon figured out what Zeus had done, so she asked him to give her the cow as a present. Zeus could not refuse without giving the game away, so he gave the cow to Hera.

Hera asked her servant Argus to make sure that Zeus kept away from the cow (Io). Argus was a giant, and made an excellent guard because he had one hundred eyes through which to watch over his charge. But Zeus was sneaky. He turned himself into a bull to visit Io and she became pregnant. Hera was so angry at Argus for letting this happen that she pulled out his eyes and used them to decorate the tail feathers of a peacock. Poor Io was then sent off to wander in the wilderness, chased on by a plague of flies sent by Hera. She wandered for a long time and eventually arrived in Egypt, where she was found by Zeus. He turned Io back into human form just in time for her to give birth to their son, Epaphus.

Hera, still in a jealous rage, kidnapped Epaphus. Io spent the rest of her days looking for her son.

MYTH AND REALITY
The Temple of Hera in Olympia was built around 600 BCE. It is one of the most famous of all Greek ruins and has appeared on Greek banknotes.

APHRODITE AND ADONIS

One day, Aphrodite, the beautiful goddess of love, was playing in the woods with her son, Eros. By accident, she cut her finger with one of Eros's arrows, and as she did this, she felt an unusual longing in her heart.

Hearing the sound of hunting dogs approaching, she stood aside as the hunters burst through the woods. That's when she saw the most handsome man she had ever seen. His beauty rivaled that of the gods. She watched as his spear flew from his hand with the accuracy of Zeus's lightning bolt.

Aphrodite asked the hunter's name and learned that he was Adonis, son of the king of Paphos. Adonis was a mighty hunter but he thought little of his beauty. Instead, he took pride in his speed and agility, and

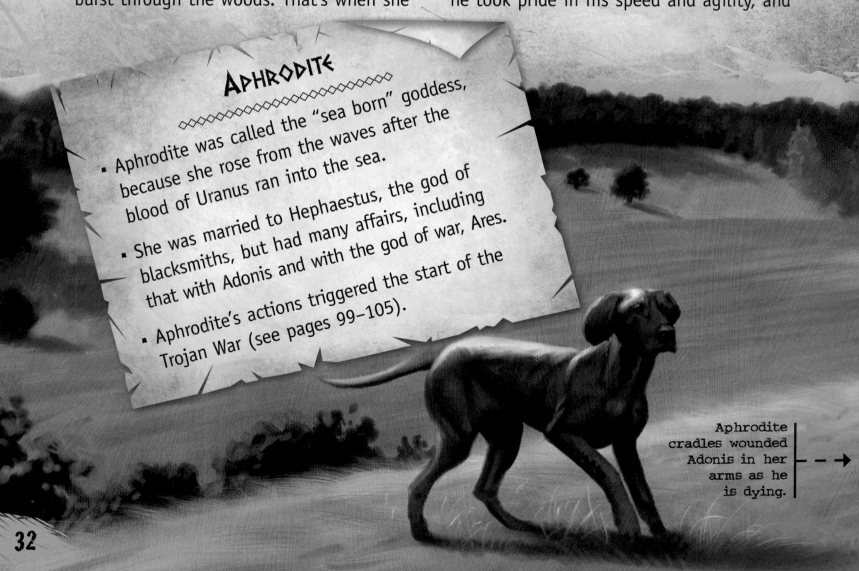

APHRODITE

- Aphrodite was called the "sea born" goddess, because she rose from the waves after the blood of Uranus ran into the sea.

- She was married to Hephaestus, the god of blacksmiths, but had many affairs, including that with Adonis and with the god of war, Ares.

- Aphrodite's actions triggered the start of the Trojan War (see pages 99–105).

Aphrodite cradles wounded Adonis in her arms as he is dying.

the accuracy of his aim. Aphrodite's heart reached out to Adonis. She knew that the wound from Eros's arrow would not heal until she had Adonis's love. She followed him everywhere he went, but Adonis still did not understand her love. Aphrodite worried that Adonis's life was full of danger, and warned him that the beasts he hunted might one day kill him, but Adonis laughed at her and thought that she was being foolish.

One day, Adonis set off to track a huge wild **boar**. Aphrodite begged him not to go, but of course his pride as a hunter was too great, and he left for the hunt.

From far away, Aphrodite heard Adonis's dogs howling a mournful cry. She ran toward the sound to find a terrible scene. Lying on the grass were the bodies of dogs that had been gored by the great boar's tusks. There also lay Adonis.

As he lay on the ground, marble-white, with the wound on his thigh flowing with blood, Adonis felt the chill of death upon him. In his last breaths he felt a great love for Aphrodite—a love stronger than life or death itself.

Aphrodite came to him and cradled his head. She reached down and kissed his cold lips as his soul slowly passed away. She prayed for Zeus to give her back her love, but there was no answer to her prayers. As she cried, her tears mixed with Adonis's blood and were turned into flowers that would forever show their unending love.

MYTH AND REALITY
The Ancient Greeks thought that humans had been taught to hunt by the gods. Hunting was a pastime of the Greek aristocracy.

ARTEMIS, GODDESS OF THE HUNT

Zeus had many love affairs with both goddesses and mortals. One of his lovers was Leto, the beautiful daughter of the Titans Coeus and Phoebe. When Hera, Zeus's wife, found out that Leto was pregnant, she forbade anyone to help her. Leto ran away and found shelter on a small island, where she gave birth to the twins Apollo and Artemis.

Artemis loved and respected wild animals. She became their guardian, and also the goddess of the hunt. Skilled with a bow and arrow, she lived in the mountains with nymphs for companions.

One day, one of her beloved deer was killed by a group of hunters, led by Agamemnon—the king of the Greek city of Mycenae. The hunters had disrespected Artemis by not offering her a **sacrifice** before hunting, as was usual.

MYTH AND REALITY

Ritual sacrifices of animals were a part of life in Ancient Greece. Animals were sacrificed to keep the gods happy—but their meat was eaten afterwards.

What's more, Agamemnon boasted that he was more skilled than Artemis with a bow and arrow. This made the goddess furious. She told Agamemnon that the only way that he could make amends for his insults was to offer his own daughter, Iphigenia, as a sacrifice.

Iphigenia was brought to the altar, but just as the priest was about to kill the girl, she vanished. In her place on the sacrificial altar was a deer. Artemis could not bear for the child to be killed after all, and so replaced her with a deer. Iphigenia was spared and later became a priestess in the Temple of Artemis.

Artemis, the huntress, substitutes a deer for Iphigenia on the sacrificial altar.

APOLLO

- Apollo was an Olympian god, the son of Zeus and Leto, and brother of Artemis.

- He was the god of healing, medicine, and prophecy. It was his job to pull the Sun across the sky in his chariot.

- He was associated with wolves, which were sometimes sacrificed in his honor.

APOLLO AND PAN'S MUSICAL CONTEST

Pan was the god of shepherds and of nature. Half human and half goat in form, he played sweet music from pipes called a **syrinx**. He was very proud of his abilities and even thought that he was a better musician than Apollo, the god of music and of the Sun.

One day, Pan challenged Apollo to a musical duel. Apollo agreed, laughing at Pan's confidence. He wanted to squash Pan's vanity, and prove to all that his music was without equal. The mountain god Tmolus was chosen to judge the contest, because the mountains are so very old and wise.

Pan and Apollo went to the mountain at the appointed time accompanied by their followers, including Midas, the king of Phrygia. Pan played first, and the music that came from his pipes was so sweet and wild that the birds flew into nearby trees to listen, fawns danced with joy, and the melody tickled the ears of rabbits. Midas thought it was the most beautiful music he had ever heard.

Then, it was Apollo's turn. He played his golden lyre so beautifully that mortals swooned, and wild creatures sat perfectly still to listen.

When Apollo stopped playing, it was as if a spell had been broken. Everyone in the audience fell to their knees and Tmolus declared Apollo the winner.

However, Midas said that he liked Pan's music more. This made Apollo furious. He told Midas that if his ears were so vulgar as to hear Pan's music as better, then they should look vulgar too. Apollo touched Midas's ears and turned them into donkey's ears—long, pointed, and furry.

PHAETHON AND APOLLO

Apollo became one of the most important gods on Olympus. He was god of music, truth, and healing, and especially of the Sun. Every day, he drove his chariot of fire across the sky bringing light to the world.

Apollo fathered many children, including Phaethon, who would boast to his friends that his father was the god of the Sun. His friends did not believe him, so to prove himself, he went to find his father at his palace. Apollo listened to his son's story and promised to grant him any wish he desired. Phaethon asked to drive the

Phaethon could not control the mighty horses that pulled Apollo's fiery chariot across the sky.

Sun chariot across the sky. Apollo argued with him, because he knew that it was a difficult and dangerous job to control the chariot. Phaethon didn't listen and insisted on this gift from Apollo.

Phaethon took the horses' reins and set off across the sky. The horses bolted and Phaethon, terrified, lost control. The chariot flew so low that it scorched the Earth, turning it into desert. Zeus came to the rescue by throwing a thunderbolt at Phaethon, killing him instantly.

MYTH AND REALITY
Ancient people did not know that the Earth moved around the Sun. Instead, they believed that the Sun was carried across the heavens every day.

PHAETHON

- Phaethon was the son of Apollo and the sea nymph Clymene.
- The name Phaethon means "the shining one" in Greek.
- After he was killed by Zeus, Phaethon was placed in the heavens and appears as the **constellation** Auriga.

DEMETER, EARTH GODDESS

Demeter was the kind and generous goddess of the harvest. She gave the world grain, fruit, and fertility. She spent more time with people than she did with the Olympians and, unlike the other gods, she could feel human emotions.

Demeter had the power of creation and destruction, and mortals relied on her to provide them with food. People worshiped her at festivals to ensure a good harvest. While she was kind, she could still show her vengeance to those who failed to give her respect. Once, she became very angry with Erysichthon, the son of the King of Thessaly.

Erysichthon was a boastful and spoiled man, who showed no respect for the gods. He desired prestige and wanted to build a great hall in which he could hold huge feasts. One day Erysichthon set out with his servants in search of good timber for the building.

Erysichthon destroys Demeter's sacred wood.

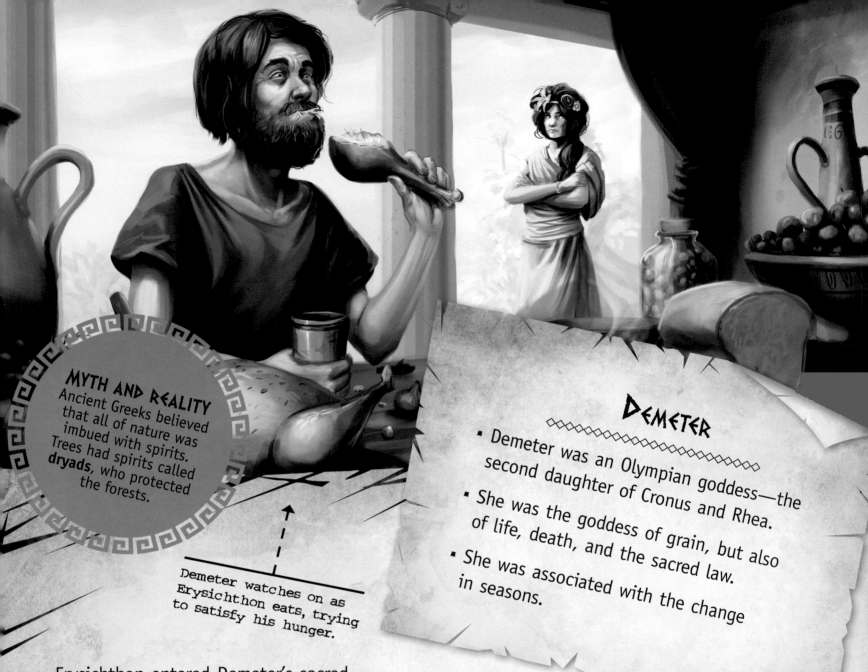

MYTH AND REALITY

Ancient Greeks believed that all of nature was imbued with spirits. Trees had spirits called **dryads**, who protected the forests.

Demeter watches on as Erysichthon eats, trying to satisfy his hunger.

DEMETER

- Demeter was an Olympian goddess—the second daughter of Cronus and Rhea.
- She was the goddess of grain, but also of life, death, and the sacred law.
- She was associated with the change in seasons.

Erysichthon entered Demeter's sacred woodland grove, and ordered his men to start chopping down the trees. A passerby warned him not to cut the trees, but Erysichthon was so full of himself that he beheaded the man for meddling.

As the men started chopping, blood began to flow from the trees, and the tree spirits cried out to Demeter. The goddess disguised herself as a priestess and came to Erysichthon. She begged him to stop destroying the grove, but Erysichthon just laughed and threatened her with his ax. Then, Demeter did a strange thing. She told him to continue cutting down the trees because he would—after all—need a dining hall. Demeter then called on Peina (Hunger) to help punish Erysichthon. Peina was happy to help teach the arrogant young man a lesson. She plagued Erysichthon with hunger, so no matter how much he ate, he was always hungry, and always eating in his dining hall. He ate so much that he spent his fortune on food, and was still hungry.

Erysichthon was left with nothing except his hunger and eventually became so hungry that he began eating his own flesh.

DEMETER AND PERSEPHONE

Demeter never married, but she had several lovers, including Zeus. Together they had two children—a son, Iacchus, and a daughter, Persephone.

Hades, the god of the Underworld, saw Persephone laughing and gathering flowers, and fell deeply in love with her. He kidnapped the beautiful goddess and locked her in a room within the Hall of Hades. Persephone's mother Demeter was so distraught that her screams could be heard in the Underworld. She wandered Earth looking for her daughter for nine days and nine nights. She did not sleep or eat.

On the tenth day, she met Hecate, the goddess of magic, who knew all about the kidnapping. Hecate told Demeter to seek out Apollo, who saw everything that happened on Earth as he crossed the sky each day. So Demeter went to Apollo. He tried to reassure her that Hades would take care of her daughter, but Demeter could not be consoled.

Hades kidnapped beautiful Persephone, and took her to the Underworld to be his wife.

Flowers bloom and plants grow in the spring, when Persephone is reunited with her mother, Demeter.

Stricken with grief and anger, Demeter stopped taking care of the land. Without her help, plants withered and died, and people on Earth faced drought and famine. A year of famine passed before Zeus went to see Demeter. She told him what had happened, and Zeus ordered Hades to return Persephone to Earth. At first Hades agreed, but he just couldn't bear to give her up, so he tricked Persephone into eating some **pomegranate** seeds. Hades knew that anyone who ate food in the Underworld could never return to the land of the living.

Finally, Zeus came up with a compromise. Persephone would spend part of the year with her mother on Earth and part of the year with Hades in the Underworld. Her time in each place would create the seasons.

While Persephone was in the Underworld, Earth would be in autumn and winter. Crops would wither and die. It would become cold and nothing would grow. When Persephone was with her mother in the spring and summer, Demeter's happiness would make plants blossom and fruits ripen.

Humans had to learn to grow crops during the time Persephone was with Demeter, and let the land rest when she was with Hades. Persephone became Hades's wife and Queen of the Underworld. Eventually, she accepted her duties as wife and queen.

HADES

- Hades was the god of death, and of funeral rites, but he was also in charge of the riches of Earth that lay underground, such as mines, and the fertility of the soil.

- He carried a pitchfork, which he drove into the ground to make earthquakes.

44

HADES AND THE UNDERWORLD

ades was the god of the Underworld. He was a somber god who liked ruling over the Land of the Dead—a place that no one was allowed to leave. When a mortal died, their soul was guided to the Underworld by Hermes, the messenger god. Getting to the Underworld meant crossing one or more rivers, for which the soul needed to pay the ferryman, Charon. If the soul had no money, it was instead destined to wander the shores of the river for 100 years before being allowed to cross.

Once across, the soul had to pass by Cerberus, Hades's fearsome watchdog. This huge animal had three heads and loved to

eat human flesh. Cerberus's job was to stop living mortals from entering the Underworld, and souls from escaping. Next, the soul would come to a junction, from which three paths led to different regions of the Underworld. The Judges of the Dead stood at this junction and decided which path the soul would take.

One path led to **Elysium**, the island of heroes. It was a paradise where men and women enjoyed a comfortable life in eternity. Another route led to the **Asphodel Fields**—a place for commoners who had not committed any serious crimes. Most souls ended up here.

A third path led to Tartarus, deep below the Underworld. It was said to be as far below the surface as the heavens were away from the Earth. Tartarus was a dark, dismal place that was feared by all. It was here that wicked mortals were sent to suffer for eternity.

← – – – – – – | Charon the ferryman carries souls across the River Styx on his boat.

MYTH AND REALITY
When people died in Ancient Greece, their relatives would often place a coin in their mouth. This was to pay the ferryman, Charon, in the Underworld.

HEPHAESTUS, GOD OF FIRE

Hephaestus was the god of fire, volcanoes, blacksmiths, and sculptors. He was a master craftsman and was not like the other gods. He was ugly, and walked with a limp.

When he was born, his mother, Hera, thought him so disgusting that she threw him out of the heavens. He fell for nine days and nights before splashing into the ocean. Hephaestus was saved and raised by Thetis and Eurynome, who hid him in an underwater cave beneath a volcano. This is where he learned his crafts.

To take revenge on Hera, Hephaestus used all his skills to make her a gift—a sparkling golden throne. Hera was enchanted by the throne, but as soon as she sat on it, she became trapped by ropes and chains. She could not get up from her seat.

The other gods implored Hephaestus to let his mother go, but he replied that he had no mother, rejecting Hera. Then, one night, Dionysus (see page 56)—the god of wine—got Hephaestus very drunk. He brought Hephaestus back to Mount Olympus, slumped on the back of a mule. Humbled, Hephaestus eventually released Hera from the throne, though he never forgave her for the way she had treated him.

MYTH AND REALITY

Craftsmen, such as blacksmiths and carpenters, had low status in Ancient Greece. They usually worked in small family-owned workshops.

Hera was trapped on a golden throne made for her by her son, Hephaestus, the god of blacksmiths and fire. - - - →

HEPHAESTUS

- Hephaestus was an Olympian god, the son of Zeus and Hera.
- He became lame when Hera threw him down from Mount Olympus.
- Hephaestus ruled over volcanoes, which were his workshops.

THE GIFT OF FIRE

After the war between the Titans and the Olympian gods, most of the defeated Titans were imprisoned in Tartarus, below the Underworld. But two Titan brothers, Prometheus and Epimetheus, were spared and remained free. They were given the job of creating animals and humans to populate Earth.

They made creatures by molding them from clay. Prometheus was clever and careful, but his brother was clumsy and thoughtless. Epimetheus was tasked by Zeus to give each creation its qualities. To some animals he gave strength and to others endurance; some received wings, others sharp claws. But by the time Prometheus had finished his best creation of all—mankind—all the qualities had been distributed. Epimetheus had kept nothing for humans.

Prometheus loved mankind, and could not bear to see them defenseless, cold, and frightened on Earth. So he went to Zeus and asked if he would give them the very special gift of fire. Zeus was angered by this question, because he had already given his gifts to be distributed among the creatures. And fire was reserved for the gods and certainly not for mankind.

But Prometheus wanted to protect mankind, and decided that if Zeus would not give the gift of fire, he would steal it. In the black of night, he took a piece of fire stuck to the wheels of Apollo's fiery chariot and gave it as a gift to mankind.

Zeus looked down on Earth and saw it glowing with firelight. The heavens shook with his anger. He knew that Prometheus had stolen the fire. As punishment, Zeus chained him to a rock far away from his beloved mankind. An eagle was sent to feed on his liver every day; and every night Prometheus's liver would grow back. Zeus vowed never to release Prometheus for disobeying him and he was left to endure this torture forever.

Prometheus took fire from the wheel of Apollo's flaming chariot, and brought it to Earth.

PANDORA'S BOX

Zeus was furious with Prometheus for stealing fire from the gods and giving it to humans (see pages 48–49). He punished Prometheus, but still wanted to take further vengeance against the human race. To do this, Zeus decided to trick Epimetheus, the foolish brother of Prometheus.

First, Zeus asked Hephaestus—the god of blacksmiths and sculptors—to form a woman from clay. This was to be the greatest and most beautiful sculpture ever created.

The woman was molded in the image of the goddesses and was given gifts from all the deities. Aphrodite gave her beauty and grace. Hera adorned her with clothes of gold and jewelry. Hermes gave her the gifts of speech, curiosity, and deceitful words.

Finally, Zeus gave the woman life and named her Pandora, which means "One Who Has All Gifts." He then sent Pandora to Epimetheus as a gift. Along with her, he sent a locked box, which was said to contain wonderful things. Athena warned Pandora never to open the box.

Pandora's box opens, unleashing unhappiness throughout the world.

Upon seeing Pandora, Epimetheus immediately fell in love. He took her home and made her his wife. Epimetheus held the keys to the box. Every day, he told his wife not to open the box. But every day Pandora grew more and more curious. Several times she took the keys from Epimetheus, but stopped herself from opening the box at the last moment.

One day, she could not fight her curiosity any longer and decided to take a peek. As soon as she opened the box, all kinds of evils were released, including plagues, diseases, and all manner of suffering for mankind. She quickly closed the lid, but it was too late. Unhappiness had spread throughout the world.

Pandora cried to her husband and told him what she had done. Just then, they heard a tiny voice from inside the box. One element had not escaped the box. Zeus came to them and told them to release the last element, but they were afraid. As they removed the lid one last time, Hope flew from the box to help mankind through the suffering that was to come.

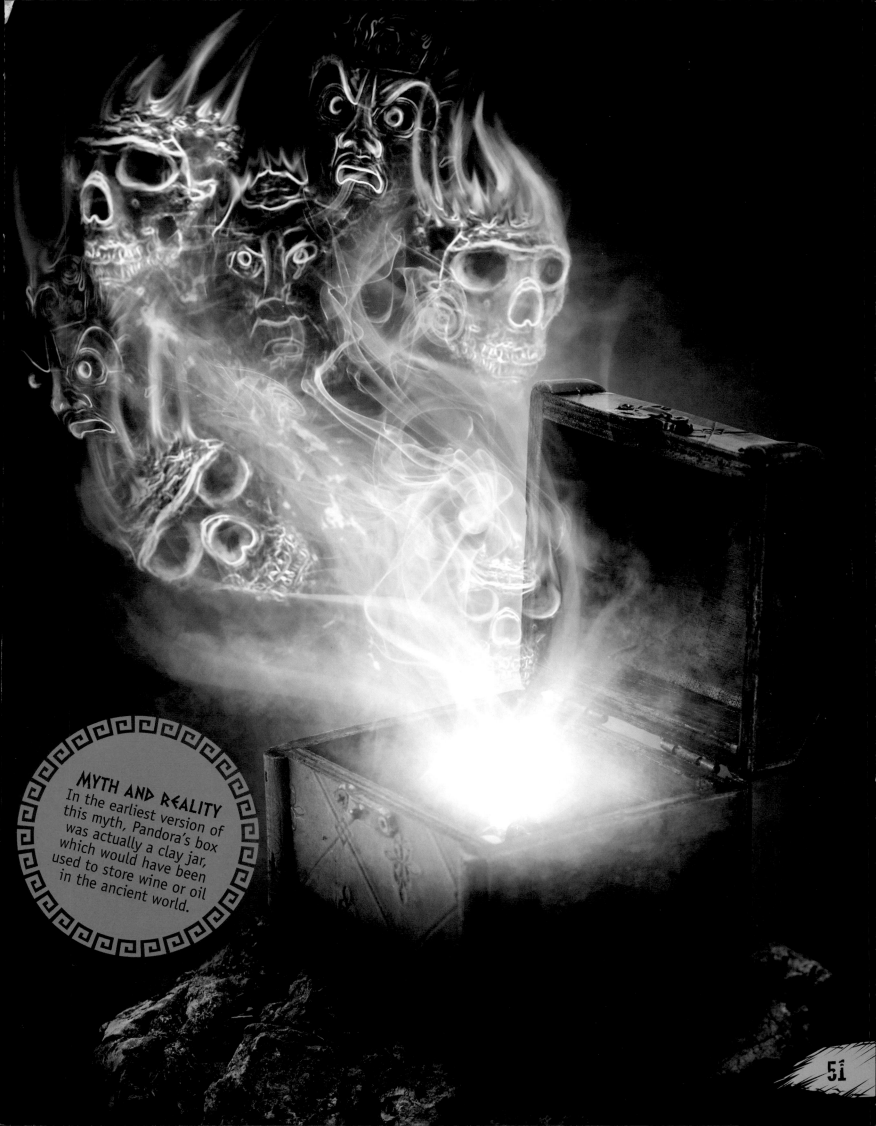

MYTH AND REALITY
In the earliest version of this myth, Pandora's box was actually a clay jar, which would have been used to store wine or oil in the ancient world.

PEACEFUL HESTIA

Hestia was the most virtuous, compassionate, and oldest of the Olympian gods. Every household worshiped her, because Hestia protected the **hearth** and home, and all the members of the family. Hestia was a modest goddess, who spent all of her time at home on Mount Olympus. She never left to roam the Earth, and unlike the other gods and goddesses, never got involved in arguments. She believed in peace and harmony.

Hestia never married, but she was courted by Poseidon and Apollo. The rivalry between these two gods grew, and threatened to develop into a full-scale war.

Hestia's honor was preserved by the braying of a donkey.

52

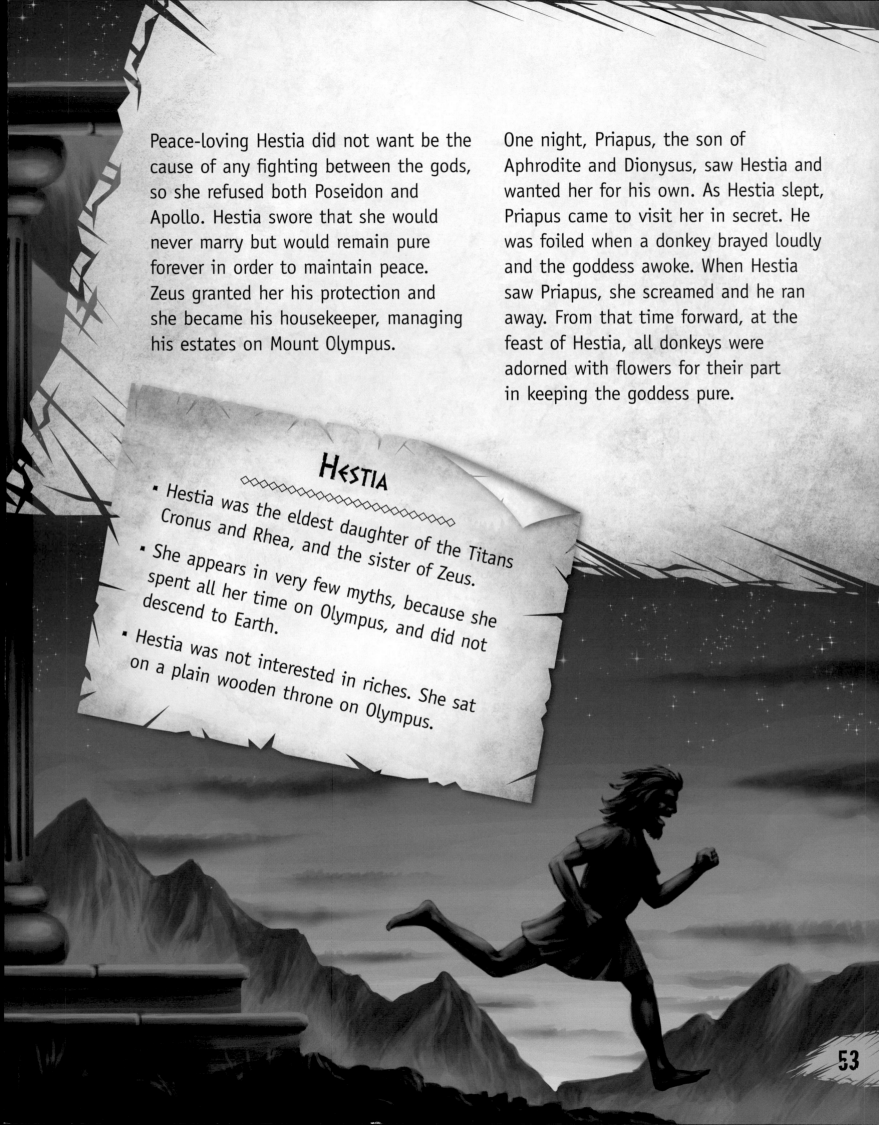

Peace-loving Hestia did not want be the cause of any fighting between the gods, so she refused both Poseidon and Apollo. Hestia swore that she would never marry but would remain pure forever in order to maintain peace. Zeus granted her his protection and she became his housekeeper, managing his estates on Mount Olympus.

One night, Priapus, the son of Aphrodite and Dionysus, saw Hestia and wanted her for his own. As Hestia slept, Priapus came to visit her in secret. He was foiled when a donkey brayed loudly and the goddess awoke. When Hestia saw Priapus, she screamed and he ran away. From that time forward, at the feast of Hestia, all donkeys were adorned with flowers for their part in keeping the goddess pure.

Hestia

- Hestia was the eldest daughter of the Titans Cronus and Rhea, and the sister of Zeus.
- She appears in very few myths, because she spent all her time on Olympus, and did not descend to Earth.
- Hestia was not interested in riches. She sat on a plain wooden throne on Olympus.

ARES

◇◇◇◇◇◇◇◇◇◇◇◇◇◇◇◇◇◇◇◇◇◇◇◇◇◇◇◇◇

- Ares was a formidable warrior who always wore armor and a helmet.

- Ares supported the Trojans—the losing side—in the Trojan War. He faced humiliation in his many defeats.

- Ares was a bitter enemy of Athena.

THE HILL OF ARES

Ares, the god of war, was the son of Zeus and Hera. He was bloodthirsty, and thrived on conflict and death. He was always looking for ways to bring more violence to the world. He cared little for justice, principles, or humanity; even his parents thought him evil and brutal.

Ares lived in Thrace, a land that bordered Greece. This land was filled with savage warriors who wielded heavy swords and were ferocious in battle. Ares fitted right in with these war-loving, battle-hungry oppressors.

Ares had a love affair with Aphrodite, one of the only Olympians who cared for the god of war. Together they had many children, but Ares favored his sons Deimos (Fear) and Phobos (Panic), who rode with him in his chariot spreading fear and panic in every battle.

Ares's daughter, Alcippe, was hurt by Halirrhothius, the son of Poseidon, god of the sea. Enraged by the crime, Ares killed Halirrhothius and in turn, Poseidon brought the god of war to trial.

The trial was held on a hill overlooking the site of the murder, with the other gods sitting in judgment. After hearing all the evidence, Ares was not punished. Later, the site became known as the Hill of Ares. It was the place where cases of murder or other serious crimes were tried.

← — — — — Ares speaks to the other gods at his trial. As usual, he carries a spear and his shield.

MYTH AND REALITY
The hill of Ares is a bare marble rock in Athens. It appears in the Bible as the place where the **apostle** and missionary, St. Paul, addressed the Athenians.

THE BIRTH OF DIONYSUS

Zeus fell in love with Semele, the mortal daughter of Cadmus of Thebes. He told her that he was a god, but he always visited her in human form. This was because any mortal who saw Zeus in his divine form would instantly die. In time, Semele became pregnant with Zeus's child.

Zeus's jealous wife, Hera, found out about the affair, and in disguise, made friends with Semele. She made Semele doubt that Zeus was really a god, and encouraged her to make him reveal his true identity.

Egged on by Hera, Semele asked Zeus to grant her a wish. Zeus agreed. Her wish was to see him in his majesty—as a god. Zeus pleaded with Semele to ask for anything else, but she would not give in. He had no choice but to reveal himself in divine form. Upon seeing him, Semele died.

Zeus was stricken with grief by Semele's death and he asked Hermes to help him save his unborn son. The two gods removed the baby from Semele's body and sewed it into Zeus's thigh. Zeus held him there until he was born. He was named Dionysus, meaning "twice born," because he was born once from Semele, and once through Zeus.

Hera was still angry and hired assassins to kill the infant. To save the child, Zeus gave him to Hermes (see pages 66–67), who in turn took the infant to safety.

Later, Dionysus was raised by nymphs, who spoiled him and fed him honey. During his stay with the nymphs Dionysus invented wine-making and later became god of wine, debauchery, and fertility.

Hermes rescues Dionysus from Hera's assassins.

DIONYSUS

- Dionysus could bring about great joy and revelry, or passion and anger, just like the wine of which he was god.

- He had supernatural powers and could bring people back from the Underworld.

- Festivals honoring Dionysus were held in the spring, when vines began to grow.

DIONYSUS AND ARIADNE

Ariadne was the daughter of King Minos of Crete, who was himself a son of Zeus. The immortal Ariadne fell in love with the Greek hero Theseus and helped him defeat the terrible Minotaur (see pages 86–87). Following this adventure, Ariadne decided to sail to Athens with Theseus and his men. She hoped to become his wife.

Breaking their journey on the island of Naxos, Theseus realized that he did not really love Ariadne, and certainly did not want to marry her. While Ariadne set off to look for fruit and bread, Theseus and his men set sail, leaving her behind on the island.

Heartbroken, and exhausted from crying, Ariadne fell asleep on the beach. Dionysus saw her sleeping and immediately fell in love. When Ariadne awoke, she found Dionysus kneeling beside her. He dried her tears and told her of his love for her. They were married soon afterwards on the same beach.

Their love was one of the strongest in Greek mythology. Even though Dionysus was the god of drunkenness and debauchery, he was one of the few gods to remain faithful to his wife. Ariadne would often be seen beside her husband, dancing with the **satyrs**, the horse-like companions of Dionysus.

MYTH AND REALITY

Dionysus was a favorite of the ancients, who developed cults and built temples to worship him. Ruins of one temple in Iria on the island of Naxos remain to this day.

The moment Dionysus falls in love with Ariadne. ├ – – – →

Ariadne

- Ariadne had four children with Dionysus, including Thoas and Oenopion, who became the kings of Lemnos and Chios.

- Ariadne was worshiped across Greece. People danced in her honor.

- She was called the "sea woman" because she was associated with the Greek islands.

POSEIDON'S PRIDE

Poseidon was the god of the seas, lakes, springs, and rivers. He had the power to bring about earthquakes, landslides, and floods. He could create savage sea storms with towering waves, and could summon up sea monsters. But, even with all of these great powers, Poseidon wasn't satisfied. He wanted to overthrow his brother, Zeus, and rule the Olympian gods.

Poseidon was a proud but quarrelsome god. He once had an argument with the wise goddess, Athena. He was angry with her because she had taught mortals how to build ships. This brought humans into Poseidon's watery realm, but he wanted the seas reserved for his creatures alone. Poseidon had also created the horse. Athena angered him again, because she had given

MYTH AND REALITY
The Ancient Greeks associated the olive tree with Athena. It became a symbol of peace and wealth, as well as hope and resurrection.

POSEIDON

- Poseidon was second only to Zeus in his strength and power.

- He could create storms, giant waves, and landslides with a wave of his trident.

- Poseidon was responsible for creating new islands from the sea, and for calming the waters for sailors.

mankind the bridle, which let them tame the horse and use it for their own purposes. The conflict between the two gods peaked when they both claimed the city of Athens as their own.

Zeus stepped in to resolve the conflict. He allowed the people of Athens to choose the god that they wanted to rule over the city by judging the gifts they gave. Poseidon—who wasn't the brightest of the gods—gave the people of Athens a saltwater spring. Athena, who was far wiser, gave them the

olive tree. Not surprisingly, the people chose Athena.

Poseidon was so disappointed that he challenged all the other gods and goddesses for their cities, too. He lost to Dionysus, Apollo, Zeus, and Hera. Despite all of these losses and Poseidon's unhappiness, he was honored and worshiped widely.

Poseidon, angry at mankind's ships.

EROS AND PSYCHE

Psyche was a mortal princess. She was among the most beautiful women on Earth. Some even said that she was fairer than Aphrodite, the goddess of love and beauty. Jealous Aphrodite sent her son, the winged god Eros, to shoot the princess with one of his magical arrows. His arrows made people fall in love, and Aphrodite planned for Psyche to fall for an ugly suitor.

However, when Eros laid eyes on Psyche, he fell deeply in love with her himself. He carried her away and they became lovers. As an immortal, Eros hid his identity from Psyche and told her never to gaze at his face. But Psyche's curiosity grew and, encouraged by her jealous sisters, she took a lamp to bed one night and looked at Eros's face. She gasped when she saw his true beauty. This woke the young god, who quickly flew away.

Aphrodite was so angry with Eros for choosing a mortal lover that she imprisoned him in her palace.

He could never see his love ever again. Psyche was heartbroken. She searched for Eros all over the Earth, but could not find him. She prayed to Aphrodite for help and the goddess gave her four near-impossible tasks to prove her love for Eros.

Aided by gods and animals, Psyche completed the first three tasks. Only one remained; this was to journey to the Underworld and bring back a box that contained the elixir of beauty. Psyche was not to open the box. Of course, Psyche was overcome by curiosity and looked inside. Instead of the elixir, the box contained Morpheus, the god of sleep and dreams, and Psyche fell into the deepest of sleeps.

Eros heard what had happened and went to his sleeping love and carried her to Mount Olympus. He begged Zeus to save Psyche. Zeus was so moved by their great love for each other that he not only saved Psyche, but made her immortal as well. The two were married and stayed together for eternity.

MYTH AND REALITY
In Greek, *psyche* means "life or spirit" and the mythical Psyche represented the female spirit. She was sometimes represented by a butterfly.

Eros takes the sleeping Psyche to Mount Olympus.

EROS

- Eros was the personification of love. He was an old god, born from Chaos.

- Eros was an annoying god, who liked to trouble the hearts of mortals.

- Eros is usually shown with wings and carrying a bow and arrow.

63

HECATE AND THE MOON

Hecate, the daughter of the Titans Perses and Asteria, was the goddess of the crossroads, the Moon, and of the mist. Hecate could see in many directions at once, because she had three heads—a lion, a horse, and a dog. This meant she could help people at crossroads in their lives, such as when they were giving birth or preparing to die.

Hecate would give money or wise advice to people, but she could also use her powers in evil ways. She was a magical goddess who seemed to have one foot in this world and one in the next.

← – – – | Three-headed Hecate holds the Moon in her hand.

Long ago, Hecate argued with the goddess Selene over who should have control over the Moon. While the two were busy arguing, the Moon vanished from the sky, and mortals became frightened. Zeus sent Apollo, the sun god, to help the two goddesses find a compromise.

Apollo suggested that they take turns controlling the Moon. Selene, who felt sorry for mortals when they could not see at nighttime, took charge of the bright side of the Moon. Hecate, who was more solitary and mysterious, took care of the Moon's dark side.

MYTH AND REALITY
The calendar used by the Ancient Greeks was based on the phases (shapes) of the Moon. There were 12 months divided into 29 or 30 days.

HERMES AND THE LYRE

A young Hermes plays his lyre to Apollo.

Hermes was the son of Zeus and Maia. Maia was one of the Pleiades (the seven daughters of the god Atlas and the nymph Pleione). Hermes was born in a cave, where his mother Maia wrapped him in swaddling clothes and laid him next to her as she slept. By noon of the next day, Hermes had grown enough to unswaddle himself and sneak out of the cave.

HERMES

- Hermes was the god of travelers, merchants, and thieves.

- He was the messenger of the gods and wore winged sandals made for him by Hephaestus.

- Hermes invented many things, including numbers and musical instruments.

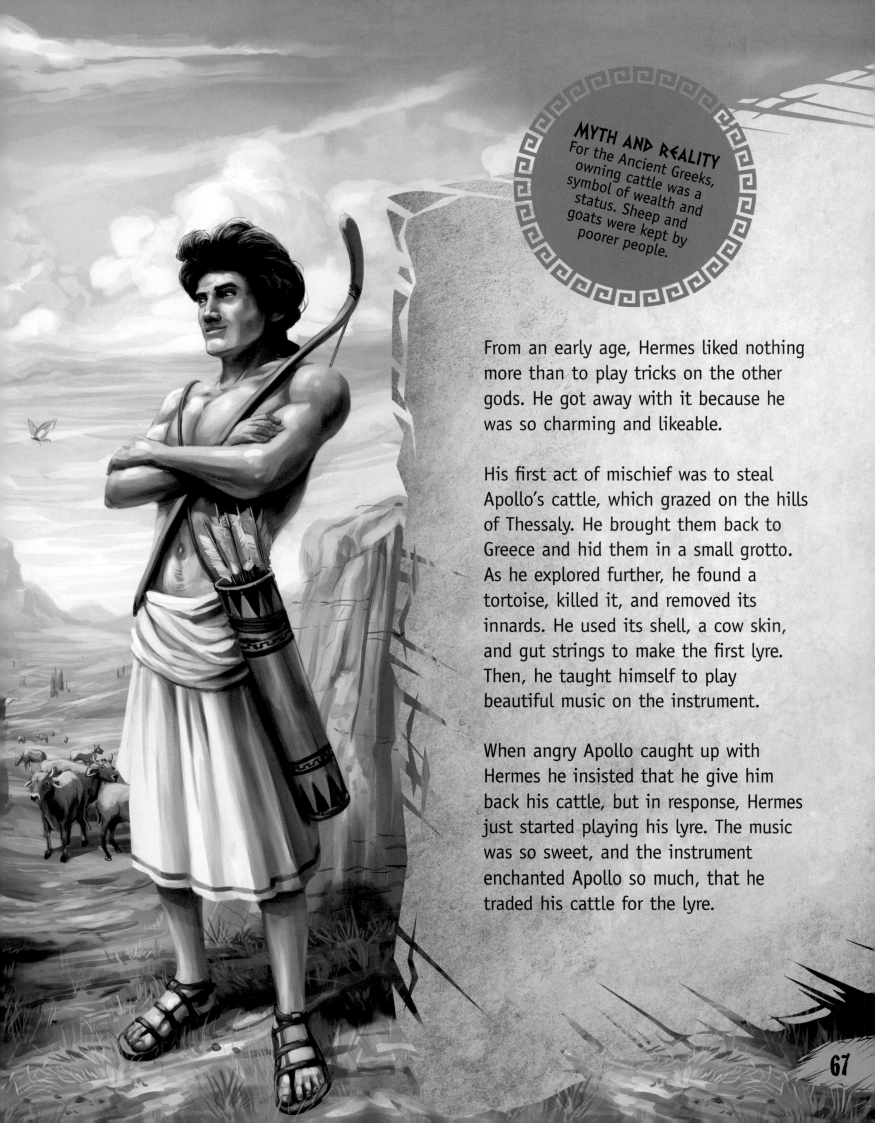

MYTH AND REALITY
For the Ancient Greeks, owning cattle was a symbol of wealth and status. Sheep and goats were kept by poorer people.

From an early age, Hermes liked nothing more than to play tricks on the other gods. He got away with it because he was so charming and likeable.

His first act of mischief was to steal Apollo's cattle, which grazed on the hills of Thessaly. He brought them back to Greece and hid them in a small grotto. As he explored further, he found a tortoise, killed it, and removed its innards. He used its shell, a cow skin, and gut strings to make the first lyre. Then, he taught himself to play beautiful music on the instrument.

When angry Apollo caught up with Hermes he insisted that he give him back his cattle, but in response, Hermes just started playing his lyre. The music was so sweet, and the instrument enchanted Apollo so much, that he traded his cattle for the lyre.

ECHO THE CHATTERBOX

Echo was a wood nymph who lived in the mountains. She had a magical voice, and her heart was as pure as her song. Echo's favorite thing was talking— she was a chatterbox.

Zeus often flirted with the wood nymphs, which made his wife, Hera, jealous. One day, Hera was chasing Zeus through the forest. Zeus spotted Echo and asked her to help him escape his wife. As Zeus hid behind a tree, Echo distracted Hera with her beautiful voice and some gossip. Day after day, the same thing happened. Zeus ran through the woods pursued by Hera, and Echo would sidetrack the goddess with her voice and chatter. When Hera found out what Echo had been doing, she punished her. Hera took away Echo's beautiful voice and allowed her only to repeat the last few words spoken to her.

Echo admires Narcissus, unable to speak to him.

One day, after she had lost her voice, Echo fell in love with a beautiful young man who would visit the woods and flirt with the nymphs. His name was Narcissus. Echo desperately wanted to tell him how she felt, but she had no voice of her own. When Narcissus spoke to her, he became annoyed by her echoed responses. He scorned Echo and told her to leave him alone, which broke her heart.

The gods wanted Narcissus to know what it felt like to love, but to not have love returned, so they cursed him. Narcissus saw his reflection in a pool of water and fell in love with this vision of beauty. When he bent down to kiss the vision, ripples in the water caused it to disappear. Every time he tried, the vision vanished, leaving him full of longing. He died of vanity—longing for the beauty of his own reflection.

One day, Pan, the god of shepherds and music, saw Echo flitting through the woods and immediately fell in love with her. But Echo had no interest in Pan, and he flew into a rage. He ordered his followers—the shepherds—to kill Echo, tear her to pieces, and spread the pieces of her body far and wide around the world.

The Earth goddess Gaia, who had always loved Echo, could not undo what Pan had done, but allowed the pieces of Echo to keep her voice. That's why today, you can hear echoes anywhere in the world.

MYTH AND REALITY

According to myth, when Narcissus died on the banks of the stream, flowers grew in his place. These are called narcissi—a type of daffodil.

Iris's colorful robes
create a rainbow.

THE HARPIES

- There were three Harpies, named Aello (wind-squall), Celaeno (storm cloud), and Ocypete (swift). Iris was their sister.

- The Harpies would carry off children and human souls in their claws.

- They lived at the entrance to the Underworld.

IRIS, GODDESS OF RAINBOWS

Iris was the daughter of the sea god Thaumas and the sea nymph Elektra. Her sisters were the evil **Harpies**—winged monsters that were spirits of the wind. They would snatch people or food from the face of the Earth.

Like her sisters, Iris too could soar on the winds like a bird. She could fly so quickly that she was made a messenger for the gods —especially Hera—taking their commands to the people on Earth. As a minor goddess, Iris remained neutral in the affairs of humans, merely carrying messages to them from the gods on Mount Olympus. Sometimes she would assume the form of a man or woman; sometimes she would reveal herself in her full glory.

Iris had long flowing hair and wore shimmering, colorful robes. The Greek mortals believed that a rainbow in the sky showed the path of Iris's journey. Her other main task was to replenish the rain clouds with water from the sea.

MYTH AND REALITY
In the Spanish language, a rainbow is called *arco iris*—which means "the arch of Iris". The word *iridescent* comes from the name of the goddess too.

ASCLEPIUS, THE HEALER

The great sun god Apollo had many lovers, one of whom was a princess of great beauty named Coronis. While pregnant with Apollo's child she fell in love with another man—a mortal prince.

Apollo, being a god, soon found out about her affair and sent his sister, Artemis, to punish Coronis. Artemis killed Coronis with her bow and arrow, and then placed her body on a pyre to burn.

At the last moment, Apollo felt guilty at killing his innocent, unborn child, so he took the baby from the body of Coronis and gave

ASCLEPIUS

- Asclepius had a wife and five children.

- He was honored in Epidaurus where a school of medicine was set up.

- One of the descendants of Asclepius was Hippocrates, who is considered to be the father of medical science.

MYTH AND REALITY
The Ancient Greeks thought that good health depended on a balance of four body fluids— blood, phlegm, yellow bile, and black bile.

it to Chiron to look after. Chiron was a wise **centaur**—half human, half horse—who was famous for his healing skills.

The rescued child of Coronis was the god Asclepius. As he grew up, he learned from Chiron how to heal people. He had exceptional skills and was able to save people who had been bitten by snakes. That's why he is often shown holding a staff with a snake wrapped around it.

Asclepius could even bring people back from the dead, which made Hades, god of the Underworld, very angry. Hades appealed to Zeus, who agreed that Asclepius was upsetting the natural order of the Universe, because mortals were not supposed to live forever. Zeus punished Asclepius by striking him with one of his thunderbolts, killing him. However, Zeus was a fair god, so he turned Asclepius into a constellation so he could live forever in the sky.

Asclepius under attack from Zeus's thunderbolts.

73

THE FATES

MYTH AND REALITY
Goddesses who spin or shape people's fate appear not just in Greek myth, but in Scandinavian and Celtic cultures.

The Fates were the three goddesses —Clotho, Lachesis, and Atropo— in charge of spinning, measuring, and cutting each person's thread of life (or lifespan). As soon as a mortal child was born, the Fates spun the life thread, which determined if that person would be good or evil, what would happen in their life, and how long they would live.

Clotho would spin a person's destiny on her spindle; Lachesis would measure the length of the thread with her staff; and Atropos would cut the thread when it was time for the life to end. The Fates watched over each mortal and made sure they followed the destiny assigned to them.

When the mortal died, the Fates arranged for their soul to be escorted to the Underworld.

People often tested the Fates by trying to control their own destinies. Sometimes the other gods tried to trick them. They usually failed. Once, Apollo got the Fates drunk in order to prevent the death of his friend, Admetus. The Fates agreed to let Admetus live only if he could find someone to take his place in death. It was Admetus's wife, Alcestis, who died for him, upon which Admetus himself no longer wanted to live.

Clotho, Lachesis, and Atropos controlling the fate of mortals.

MYTH AND REALITY
Orion is one of the most visible constellations in the night sky. It contains the bright stars Rigel and Betelgeuse.

THE SEVEN SISTERS

O ne day, on the island of Chios, the handsome hunter Orion fell in love with the Pleiades. They were the seven daughters of the sea nymph Pleione and the Titan Atlas (see page 15). The sisters were named Maia, Elektra, Alcyone, Taygete, Asterope, Celaeno, and Merope.

Orion decided that he must have all seven sisters for his wives and he pursued them all over the Earth. Zeus took pity on the young girls and turned them into doves. They flew up to the heavens and are still there as stars today, pursued by the constellation of Orion in the night sky.

←— — — Zeus turns the seven sisters into doves.

ORION

- Orion was the son of the sea god Poseidon. His father gave him the gift of being able to walk on water.

- He was famed for being strong and handsome, and for his hunting skills.

- Orion appears in the great story, *The Odyssey*, when Odysseus sees his shade (soul) in the Underworld.

THE NINE MUSES

The **Muses** were the daughters of Zeus and the Titan Mnemosyne— the goddess of memory. Zeus spent nine nights in a row with Mnemosyne, and their love produced nine daughters. Mnemosyne gave her daughters to the Nymph Eufime and the god Apollo to raise. Each of the nine beautiful Muses dedicated her life to one aspect of the arts. They lived in the woods and were often seen holding hands and dancing in a circle to show that all of the arts were connected. The Muses inspired writers, artists, and musicians, who would dedicate their work to them, or appeal for their help in producing their art.

THE MUSES

MYTH AND REALITY
The places dedicated to the Muses were known as *mouseions*, from which comes the word "museum."

- **Calliope** inspired epic poems.
- **Euterpe** inspired poetry that was accompanied by music.
- **Terpsichore** encouraged dancers.
- **Clio** was responsible for history.
- **Thalia** was dedicated to comedy.
- **Melpomene** inspired drama and tragedy.
- **Erato** inspired love poems.
- **Polyhymnia** was connected to religious and sacred music.
- **Urania** was the muse of astronomy.

The nine Muses, dancing in a circle and connecting the arts.

Heracles, a mortal,
carrying out his
twelve labors (see
pages 130–141).

MYTHS OF THE MORTALS

While the gods of Ancient Greece are central to many, many myths, there are plenty of stories about mortals, too. Some mortals were everyday people. Others had extraordinary skills, such as courage, strength, or cunning, or had been given divine qualities by the gods.

Mortal heroes often set out on adventures or quests, where they faced grave dangers, or accomplished near-impossible tasks. The heroes helped humanity and were sometimes guided or hindered by the gods.

The next pages tell the stories of these heroes—mortals like Jason, who went in search of the golden fleece, a symbol of power and authority; Odysseus, a great hero of the Trojan War; and Heracles who killed the Nemean Lion and journeyed to the Underworld.

MYTH AND REALITY
In Greek myths, mortals could become elevated into gods through great deeds, marriage, or by chance. This process was called "apotheosis."

SISYPHUS AND THE BOULDER

One day, Sisyphus saw Zeus kidnap Aegina, the daughter of the river god Asopus. Sisyphus promised Zeus that he wouldn't reveal where she was, but when old Asopus came looking for her, Sisyphus made a deal. He would tell Asopus where to find Aegina if he would create an eternal spring to provide water for the city of Corinth. Asopus agreed and the deal was done.

Zeus was so angry with Sisyphus for betraying his godly secrets that he sent him to Hades, the Underworld, and gave him a terrible punishment.

Zeus made Sisyphus roll a heavy boulder up a steep hill. Every time Sisyphus got close to the top of the hill, his strength would fail, and the boulder would roll back down. Sisyphus had to start again. This punishment continued for eternity.

Sisyphus carrying out his punishment, while Zeus watches. - - - ->

MYTH AND REALITY
The Isthmian Games were founded by Sisyphus. These athletic and artistic competitions were open to all Greeks and rivaled the Olympic Games.

SISYPHUS

- Sisyphus was the king of Corinth in the Peloponnese area of Greece.

- He was said to be the wisest and most cunning of all mortals.

- He founded the Isthmian games—a famous athletic and artistic contest.

CADMUS AND THE DRAGON

When Zeus kidnapped Europa, the daughter of the king of Tyre, the king sent his four sons to rescue her. They searched far and wide, but could not find Europa. Three of the sons gave up their search and only the eldest of the four, Cadmus, continued. He visited the Oracle at Delphi for advice. She told him to stop looking for Europa, and instead to follow a cow with a moon-shaped mark on its side. He was to follow the cow until it lay down, and on that spot, Cadmus was to found a new city.

Cadmus about to kill the dragon.

Cadmus did as he was told by the Oracle. Eventually the cow lay down, exhausted. Cadmus decided to sacrifice the cow to Athena to thank her for bringing him safely to this spot.

He sent his men to a spring to collect pure water for the sacrifice, but they failed to return. Cadmus went to find them and encountered a great dragon—the son of Ares, the god of war—that had killed his men. Cadmus sprang into action and crushed the dragon's head with a rock. Athena then appeared and told Cadmus to bury the dragon's teeth in the ground. As soon as he did this, the teeth grew into warriors who fought one another, until only five remained alive. These men helped Cadmus found a new city, which came to be called Thebes.

Cadmus had to serve Ares for eight years to make up for killing his beloved dragon. At the end of this time, Athena made Cadmus king of Thebes.

MYTH AND REALITY

Ancient Thebes was a great city that rivaled Athens. It was surrounded by a wall with seven gates.

THESEUS AND THE MINOTAUR

King Minos, the son of Zeus and the goddess Europa, was a powerful ruler who lived in a giant palace on his home island of Crete. Minos had once tried to trick the sea god Poseidon. As a punishment, Minos's wife, Pasiphae, had given birth to a monstrous child, which had the head of a bull and the body of a human. Minos was so ashamed of this awful creature, the Minotaur, that he kept it trapped in a complicated **labyrinth** (or maze) beneath the ground.

Minos's son, Androgeus, was killed by the Athenians, who were jealous of his athletic skills. Minos was furious and threatened to send a plague on Athens unless its people made a sacrifice in return. He demanded that seven young Athenian men and seven young women be sent to him every year. These poor souls would be sent into the labyrinth and be devoured by the Minotaur as a sacrifice.

Theseus, son of the king of Athens, volunteered to be part of the sacrifice, but really he planned to kill the Minotaur. Upon arriving in Crete, Theseus met Ariadne, the daughter of Minos (see page 58). She fell deeply in love with Theseus and vowed to help him defeat the Minotaur and escape the labyrinth.

As Theseus and the other Athenians were sent into the maze, Ariadne gave Theseus a spool of thread. She told him to unravel it as he went into the Labyrinth. He would then be able to find his way back out of the labyrinth by following the thread.

Theseus came face to face with the giant Minotaur, and after a brutal fight, he killed the monster. With the help of Ariadne's thread, Theseus was able to lead the Athenian prisoners out of the labyrinth. Theseus saved Athens from the plague and became a hero.

Ariadne gives Theseus a spool of thread and explains her plan.

THESEUS

- Theseus was a great Greek hero, who possessed strength, wisdom, and cunning.

- He was the younger cousin of Heracles.

- Theseus helped to make Athens into a powerful city and led its army many times to victory against its enemies.

JASON

- Jason appears in many stories, including Dante's 14th century *Divine Comedy*.

- The crew that Jason assembled for the *Argo* included Heracles, Orpheus, and the sons of the North Wind who could fly.

Jason carries Hera, disguised as an old woman, across a river.

JASON AND THE GOLDEN FLEECE

There once lived a man named Aeson who was the rightful king of Iolcus. But Aeson's evil brother, Pelias, was hungry for power and stole the kingdom from Aeson. To keep hold of the kingdom, Pelias threw his brother into a dungeon and killed his children so that they could not challenge him in the future.

But one of Aeson's children—Jason— escaped, and was raised in safety by Chiron, a wise centaur. Jason's uncle Pelias, still worried that he would be overthrown, went to seek the advice of an oracle, or prophet. The oracle warned him that he would one day be challenged for his kingdom by a man wearing one shoe—a prophecy that was soon to unfold.

When Jason was a young man, he returned to Iolcus to reclaim the throne. On his journey, Hera appeared to Jason as an old woman and asked him to carry her across a river. As he did so, he lost one of his sandals, which was carried away by the waters of the river.

So when Jason appeared before Pelias in Iolcus, he was wearing just one shoe. Pelias was horrified. He told Jason that he could take the throne, but only if he completed a near-impossible task—to find and return the legendary Golden Fleece. This was the fleece of a winged ram that lived in Colchis—now part of Turkey. It was a symbol of kingship.

Jason gathered a crew of Greece's greatest heroes, including Heracles and Orpheus, to help him on his quest, and built a ship under the direction of the goddess Athena. The ship was called the *Argo* and the crew were known as the Argonauts.

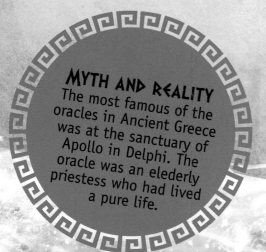

MYTH AND REALITY
The most famous of the oracles in Ancient Greece was at the sanctuary of Apollo in Delphi. The oracle was an elederly priestess who had lived a pure life.

Jason's heroic companions boarded *Argo* and set sail for Colchis, where the Golden Fleece could be found. Among their many adventures, they fought with six-armed giants in the land of Propontis, and landed at Bithynia. Here they met the blind king, Phineus, who could predict the future. Phineus was tormented by flying she-monsters called Harpies (see page 71), who continually stole his food. The Argonauts chased away the Harpies. In gratitude, the king gave Jason good advice on how to proceed on his journey.

Heeding Phineus, the Argonauts sailed safely between the Clashing Rocks—huge cliffs on either side of the sea that pressed together, crushing any passing ships. Finally, they arrived in Colchis. Here, they were met by the king, Aetes, who considered the golden fleece to be his own property. Aetes told Jason that he could take the fleece only if he completed certain tasks. Jason was helped in these tasks by the goddesses Hera and Athena, and by the King's daughter Medea, who had magical powers, and who was in love with Jason.

The king asked Jason to harness his bulls—creatures that breathed fire and had razor-sharp hooves—and then plow, sow, and harvest a field in a single day. Medea helped Jason by giving him a magical oil that he smeared over his body. This made him immune to the fire and slashing hooves of the bulls. The seeds that Jason scattered were no ordinary seeds—each one grew into an armed warrior. Medea told Jason to throw a rock at the feet of one warrior. This warrior, thinking that another warrior had insulted him, began to fight, and soon all the warriors had destroyed one another.

Even though Jason had completed Aetes's tasks, the king still refused to hand over the fleece. Jason knew that he would have to steal it from under the nose of a ferocious dragon that guarded the fleece. Once again, Medea helped Jason by giving the dragon a sleeping potion. Jason grabbed the fleece while the dragon slept.

With his task complete, Jason set sail back to Iolcus with the fleece tied to his mast. He took Medea with him as his wife.

On his return, Jason met his father Aeson who, by now, was dying. Medea used her potions to make Aeson young again. On seeing this, Pelias wanted to become younger, too. Medea told Pelias that she could do this by chopping him up into pieces and heating him in a pot with special herbs. Pelias agreed, but Medea didn't add the magical herbs, and the evil king died.

When the people of Iolcus found out how Pelias had been killed, they were horrified and exiled both Jason and Medea from their land forever.

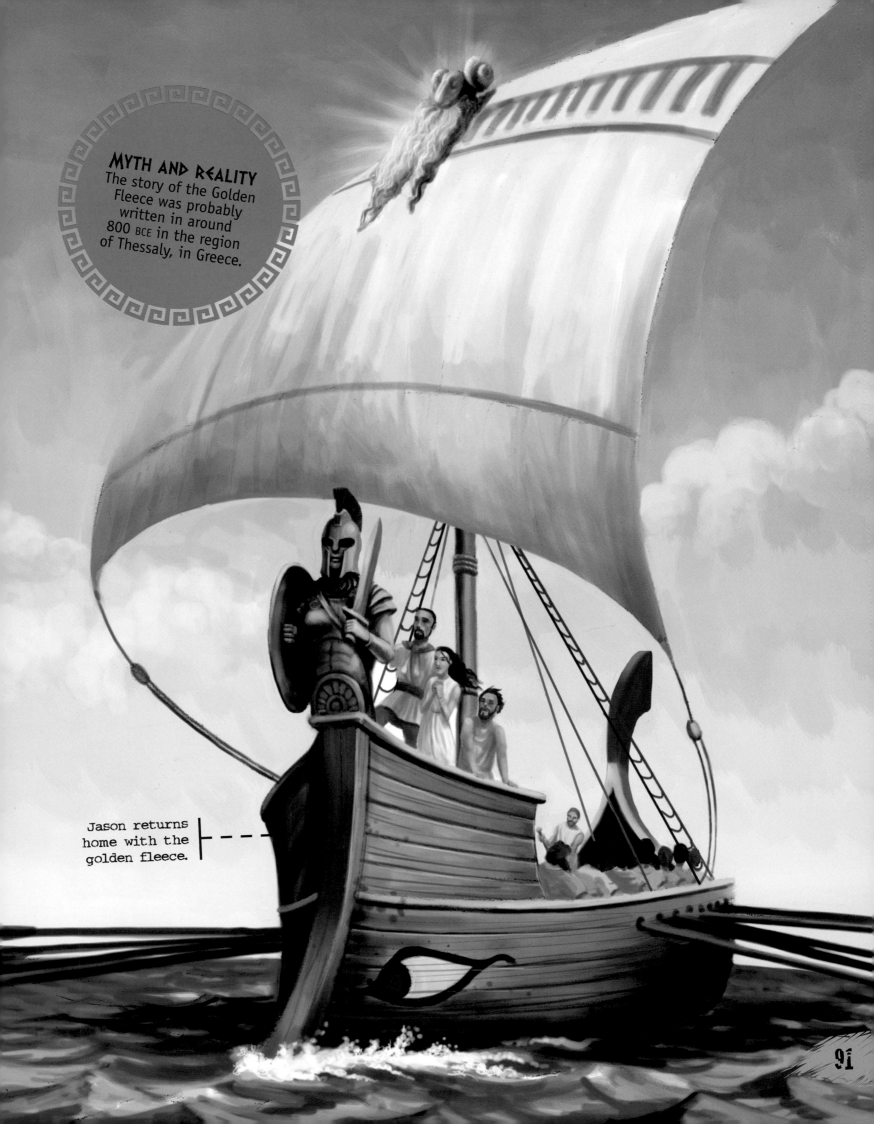

PYGMALION AND GALATEA

ygmalion was a handsome and talented sculptor who lived on the island of Cyprus. He lived for his art and saw beauty only in his own creations. One day, Pygmalion found the most perfect piece of **ivory** and worked for days, shaping it into a statue of a dazzlingly beautiful woman. She was so expertly carved that she seemed very lifelike.

Pygmalion fell in love with his creation and spent days and nights staring at her. He thought her so lovely that he clothed her, gave her jewels, and named her Galatea, which means "sleeping love." Pygmalion longed for Galatea to become human—flesh and blood—and wanted her for his wife.

← − − − − − | Pygmalion praying that the statue of Galatea would become human.

Pygmalion went to a festival to honor the goddess of love, Aphrodite (see page 32). He prayed to the goddess, asking her to give life to Galatea.

Aphrodite was moved by his prayers and she went to see the sculpture of Galatea for herself. She thought it was like looking at her own reflection and was so flattered that she brought the statue to life.

When Pygmalion came home, he kissed the statue and was surprised by her warmth. He began showering her with kisses and, as he did so, the ivory became flesh. Galatea told him that it was his deep love for her that convinced Aphrodite to answer his prayers.

Pygmalion and Galatea married and invited Aphrodite to be the guest of honor at their wedding. They never forgot to honor and pay tribute to the goddess, and she continued to bless them with happiness and love.

MYTH AND REALITY
Festivals to worship the gods were an important part of life for the Ancient Greeks. They usually involved dancing, singing, feasting, and sacrifices.

HEROK PERSEUS

King Acrisius of Argos was told by an oracle that he would be killed by his daughter's child. So when his daughter Danae became pregnant and gave birth to a son—Perseus—the king locked them both in a chest, which he cast out to sea. Poseidon, the god of the sea (see page 21), took pity on Danae and her son, and the chest washed up undamaged on the island of Seriphos. The island's king, Polydectes, wanted Danae as his wife, but Danae had no desire for the king. Perseus protected his mother from the king's advances. Polydectes plotted to get rid of Perseus by sending him on a mission he thought impossible—to bring him the head of the monstrous Medusa.

PERSEUS AND MEDUSA

Medusa was a gorgon, one of three sisters who had serpents for hair, long, sharp teeth, and claws. Anyone who looked at Medusa would turn to stone. Perseus knew that he needed help if he was to succeed in returning with the gorgon's head.

MYTH AND REALITY
Argos is one of the oldest cities in Greece. It has been inhabited for at least 7,000 years.

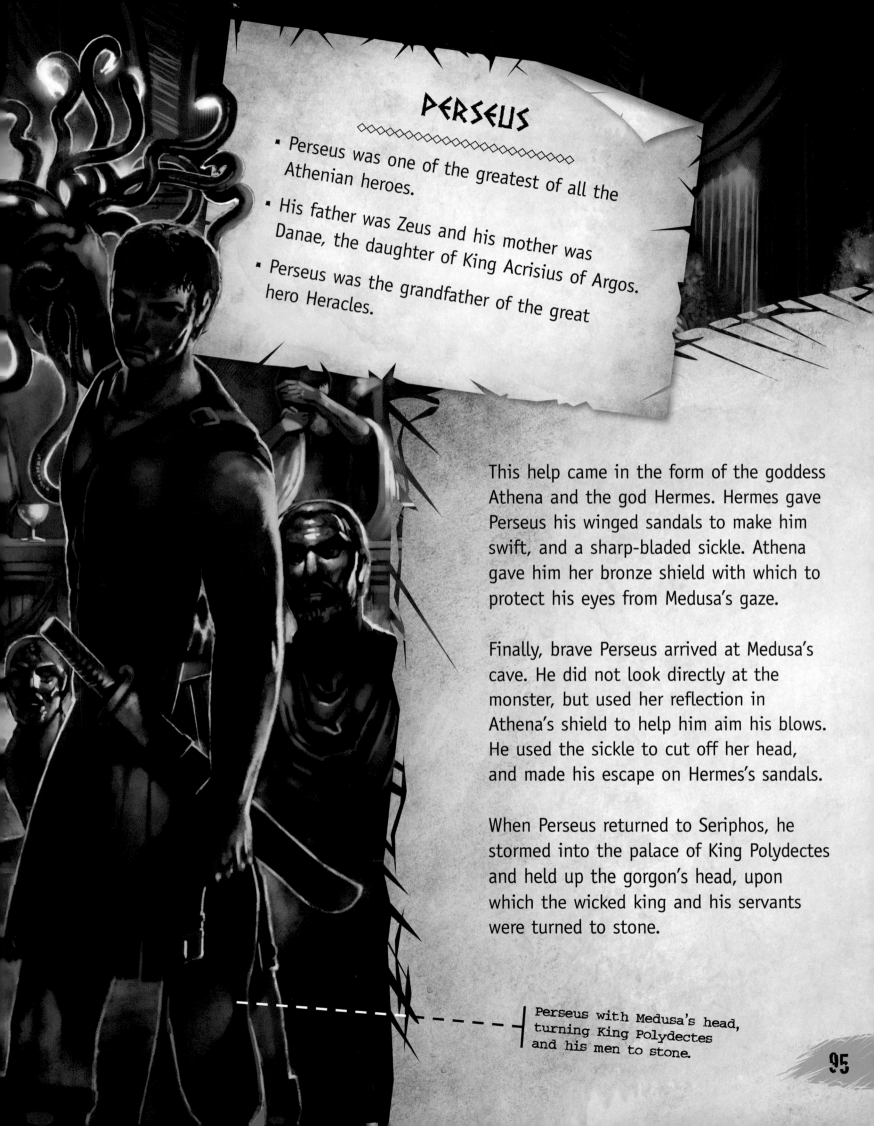

PERSEUS

- Perseus was one of the greatest of all the Athenian heroes.
- His father was Zeus and his mother was Danae, the daughter of King Acrisius of Argos.
- Perseus was the grandfather of the great hero Heracles.

This help came in the form of the goddess Athena and the god Hermes. Hermes gave Perseus his winged sandals to make him swift, and a sharp-bladed sickle. Athena gave him her bronze shield with which to protect his eyes from Medusa's gaze.

Finally, brave Perseus arrived at Medusa's cave. He did not look directly at the monster, but used her reflection in Athena's shield to help him aim his blows. He used the sickle to cut off her head, and made his escape on Hermes's sandals.

When Perseus returned to Seriphos, he stormed into the palace of King Polydectes and held up the gorgon's head, upon which the wicked king and his servants were turned to stone.

Perseus with Medusa's head, turning King Polydectes and his men to stone.

PERSEUS AND ANDROMEDA

While bringing Medusa's head back to the court of King Polydectes, Perseus was involved in another adventure. As he soared over the sea, carried through the air on the winged sandals of Hermes, Perseus spotted a beautiful young woman, seemingly asleep on the rocks overlooking the water.

The woman was Andromeda, the daughter of the king of Joppa. Her mother, Cassiopeia, was so proud of her daughter's beauty that she declared her to be more beautiful than the Sea Nymphs—the female water spirits who accompanied the god Poseidon.

The Sea Nymphs were so offended by Cassiopea's claims that they complained to Poseidon. They insisted that he punish Cassiopea. So Poseidon sent a sea monster, Cetus, to attack the coast. The king asked an oracle what he could do to stop this. The oracle told him that the only way to stop Cetus from ravaging Joppa was to offer his daughter, Andromeda, as a sacrifice. The king ordered her to be chained to the cliff by the sea to await the arrival of Cetus. This was when Perseus spotted Andromeda alone on the rocks.

When Cetus, the terrible sea monster, arrived to take Andromeda, Perseus attacked and killed the beast with Hermes's sickle. Perseus was enchanted by Andromeda's beauty and they fell in love. They stayed together even after their deaths because Athena placed the lovers in the sky as constellations.

MYTH AND REALITY
Whales and dolphins are called cetaceans, after Cetus, although they have little in common with the monstrous sea serpent.

Perseus saves Andromeda from the terrifying sea monster, Cetus. ├ - - - →

The gods watch over a battle between the Greeks and the Trojans.

THE TROJAN WAR

The Trojan War was a long, bloody, and destructive conflict that caused many deaths and tragedies. It was a time when soldiers became heroes, and heroes became gods. It is one of the most significant happenings in the myths of Ancient Greece.

The war lasted for ten years, in which time Greek forces battled with the Trojan army from the great city of Troy. The gods and goddesses took great interest in the war. Many of them chose sides and helped their favorites. Some gods—notably Poseidon, Hera, and Athena—supported the Greeks, while the Trojans gained help from Aphrodite, Apollo, Artemis, and Ares. Hades, Hestia, Demeter, and Zeus remained neutral.

The conflict all began at the wedding of Peleus and Thetis—the parents of Achilles, who was to become one of the greatest Greek heroes.

MYTH AND REALITY

The story of the Trojan War is told in an epic poem called the *Iliad*, which was written by Homer in around 850 BCE.

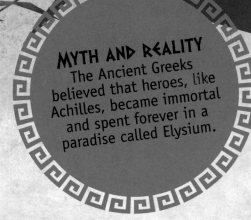
HEROIC ACHILLES

Achilles was one of the greatest Greek warriors. When he was an infant, his mother, the sea nymph Thetis, wanted to make him invincible. She did this by dipping him into the waters of the Styx—the river between the world of the living and the Underworld. As she lowered Achilles into the river, Thetis held him by his heel, and so this part of his body always remained vulnerable.

A prophet had warned the Greeks that they could not win the Trojan War without the help of Achilles. So Odysseus, one of the Greek leaders, persuaded him to join the Greek forces under the command of King Agamemnon.

In the tenth year of the war, Achilles and Agamemnon had a big argument. Achilles refused to keep fighting, and without him the Greeks began to lose the war. Achilles's friend, Patroclus, tried to fool the Trojans into thinking that Achilles was still fighting in order to frighten them. He borrowed Achilles's armor and went into battle, but was killed by Hector, the son of Troy's king, Priam. Hearing about the death of his good friend, Achilles rejoined the war with renewed anger. He killed countless Trojans and finally slew Hector, dragging his dead body behind his chariot as he drove around the walls of Troy. The Trojans were horrified and vowed revenge.

Hector's brother, Paris, fired an arrow, which, guided by the god Apollo, struck Achilles in the one spot where he was vulnerable—his heel. It killed him instantly. His mother and the nine Muses attended his funeral and made sure that he was taken to Elysium where he could live out eternity as a hero.

Achilles, fatally wounded by an arrow in his heel ⊢ - - →

ACHILLES

- Achilles is one of the main characters in *The Iliad*, the epic poem by Homer.

- He was the son of Peleus, the king of the Myrmidons, a tribe of fearless warriors.

- He was known for his loyalty and courage, but also his obstinacy.

MYTH AND REALITY
Troy was an ancient city, and is now an archaeological site in Turkey. The Trojan war probably took place around the 13th century BCE.

THE TROJAN HORSE

After ten years of fighting the Trojan War, morale among the Greek forces was very low. The Greeks knew they had to get inside the walls of Troy somehow to bring the conflict to an end. So, they came up with a cunning plan.

The Greeks built a large, hollow, wooden horse and left it outside the gates of Troy. Then they pretended to give up the fight and sail away. One of the Greeks—Sinon—stayed behind and persuaded the Trojans that the horse was a gift from the Greeks—an offer to the goddess Athena. Some of the Trojans thought the horse was some kind of trick, but most were happy because they thought they had won the war. They opened the gates, pulled the horse within the city walls, and celebrated their victory over the Greeks.

What the Trojans didn't realize was that the horse was hollow and filled with Greek soldiers, including Odysseus and Diomedes.

Under the cover of night, the Greeks snuck out of the horse and opened the gates for the rest of the Greek army, which had sailed back to Troy. The Greeks flooded into Troy, destroyed the city, and ended the war once and for all.

← — — — — — — — | Greek warriors secretly leaving the Trojan horse.

KING MIDAS

Midas was the king of a land called Phrygia. One day, his men found a drunken satyr sleeping in Midas's vineyard. They captured the satyr, tied him up, and brought him to Midas to decide his fate. The King recognized the satyr as Silenus, a helper of Dionysus (see page 56), the god of wine and fertility, and so set him free.

Dionysus was very grateful to Midas for the safe return of the satyr Silenus.

King Midas transforms his daughter into a golden statue.

As a reward, Dionysus offered Midas a reward of anything he wished. Midas asked for the gift to turn anything he touched into gold. Dionysus granted his wish.

At first, Midas was thrilled because he thought he would become the richest man in the world. However, his joy soon became hollow. When he picked a rose that he wanted to smell, the flower turned to solid gold that had no fragrance. Hungry, he picked up a grape, and then a piece of bread, but they both turned to gold before he could eat them. And when he went to hug his daughter, he accidentally transformed her into a golden statue.

Midas prayed to Dionysus to take the gift away. The god took pity on the king and sent him to the river to wash his hands. When Midas returned, everything he touched returned to normal. The king was so relieved that he decided to share his fortune with his people.

MYTH AND REALITY
The Ancient Greeks used coins made from gold and silver. They usually had a portrait of a god or hero on one side, and an emblem of their city on the other.

107

THE ADVENTURES OF ODYSSEUS

At the end of the Trojan War, the Greek hero Odysseus longed to return to his wife Penelope and his home on the island of Ithaca. He set sail from Troy with his men. Their journey home was to unexpectedly take ten years and involve many adventures.

GREEDY IN ISMARUS

After leaving Troy, the winds swept Odysseus and his twelve ships to Ismarus, city of the Ciconians. Here, his men became carried away by greed. They killed the inhabitants, stole their possessions, and plundered the land. As the men drank the local wine, the Ciconians gathered reinforcements. And as the men feasted on the beach, the Ciconian warriors attacked. Odysseus's men were outnumbered, and before they could escape on their ships, more than 70 of them were killed.

THE LOTUS EATERS

Once at sea again, Odysseus and his men faced a terrible storm. After many days they landed on an island, where they found the people to be kind and generous. The natives gave the men fruits from the lotus plant to eat. On eating the fruits, the men lost all their desire to return home, and could think only of staying on the island and eating forever. Odysseus had to force them back onto the ships, and tie them down before they could set sail again.

The angry Ciconians about to attack Odysseus's men. ├ - - - →

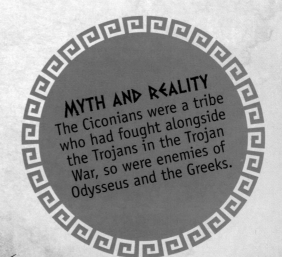

MYTH AND REALITY
The Ciconians were a tribe who had fought alongside the Trojans in the Trojan War, so were enemies of Odysseus and the Greeks.

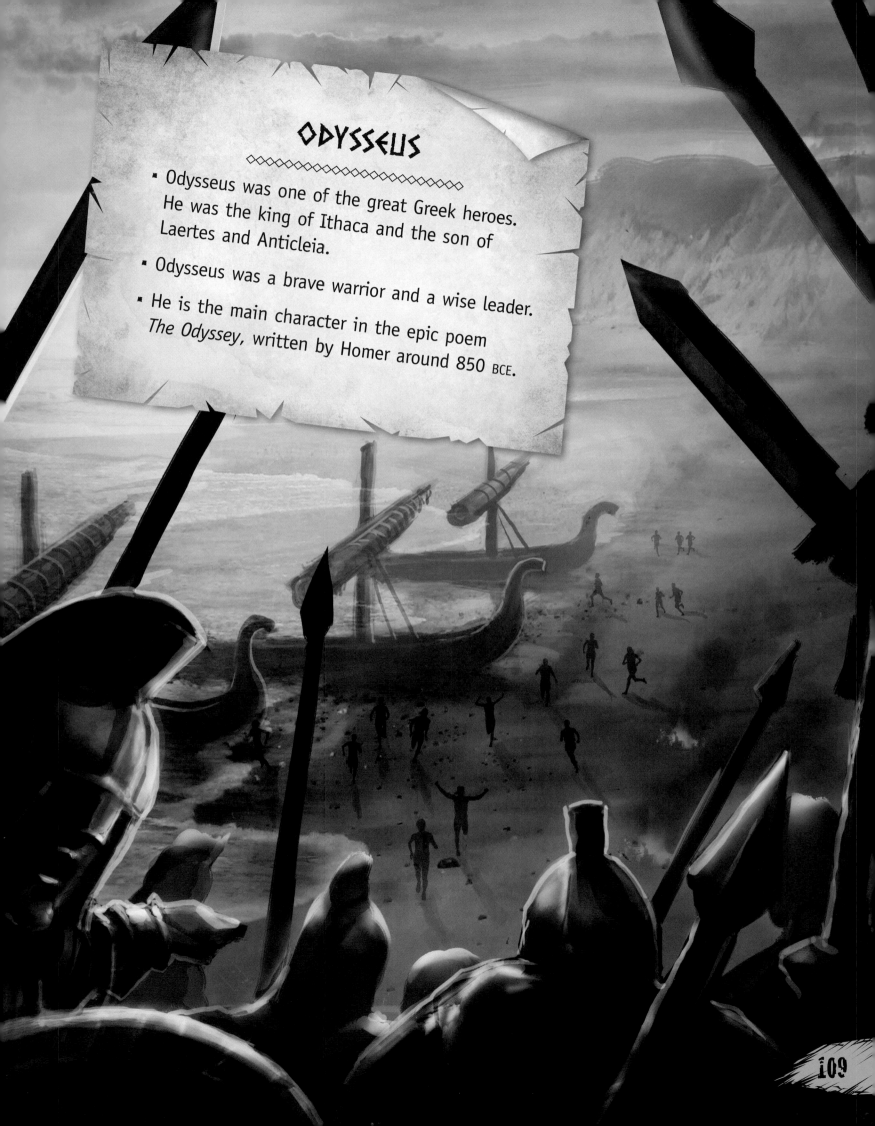

ODYSSEUS

- Odysseus was one of the great Greek heroes. He was the king of Ithaca and the son of Laertes and Anticleia.

- Odysseus was a brave warrior and a wise leader.

- He is the main character in the epic poem *The Odyssey*, written by Homer around 850 BCE.

CYCLOPS'S CAVE

After sailing through the night, Odysseus and his men stopped at a small island, populated with wild goats. The men feasted on the goats and filled their bellies. They then set off to explore, and soon discovered a cave in which was a pen of goats and many big wheels of cheese.

The crew snuck into the cave, intending to steal the goats and the cheese, but to their horror, the occupant of the cave returned. This was Cyclops, son of Poseidon, god of the sea. Cyclops was so large that he blotted out the sun, and his one huge eye stared out from the center of his forehead.

Cyclops pulled a huge boulder across the opening to the cave and trapped the men inside. He asked where the men had come from, and Odysseus told him the tale of the Trojan War and of their difficult journey home. Odysseus asked Cyclops to extend them his hospitality, as would be expected by Zeus; Cyclops, though, exclaimed that he was stronger than Zeus. To prove his point, he grabbed two of Odysseus's men and ate them. Odysseus and his men were imprisoned for future meals.

In the morning, Cyclops ate two of the men for breakfast. Then, he left to tend to his sheep. Odysseus made a plan. He sharpened a wooden pole. When Cyclops returned, Odysseus gave him wine to wash down his feast. Cyclops drank it in one gulp and demanded more. He drank too much and fell asleep. While he was sleeping, Odysseus and his men drove the sharpened pole into Cyclops's eye.

The Cyclops woke up in tremendous pain, and almost blind. While he cried out and raged, Odysseus and his men were able to escape from the cave by hanging on to the bellies of the sheep as they left.

Odysseus about to strike Cyclops as he slept.

CYCLOPS

- Cyclops was a member of a race of primitive giants—The Cyclopes—which had been released from Tartarus by Zeus.

- The name Cyclops means "circle-eye."

- According to some myths, the Cyclopes helped the god Hephaestus at his forge.

THE BAG OF WINDS

When Odysseus and his men set sail from the island of Cyclops there was very little wind to sail by. Odysseus asked for help from King Aeolus, ruler of the winds, who lived on a floating island. The king gave Odysseus a bag that contained all the winds of the Earth to help them on their journey.

Odysseus summoned up a westerly wind to push his ship back home and within a few days, they spotted their island, Ithaca. However, the crew grew suspicious. They thought that the bag that King Aeolus had given Odysseus held a fortune in gold and silver, rather than just the winds, and they wanted their share. The men opened the bag and in doing so released all of the winds! This created a huge storm that blew them all the way back to King Aeolus. This time, the king of the winds refused to help them.

← – – – – – ┤ The Laestrygonians attacking Odysseus and his men

GIANT CANNIBALS

Without any wind to fill their sails, Odysseus and his men began to row their ships across the sea. They rowed until they reached the city of Telepylus, which was the home of the Laestrygonians. The Laestrygonians were a race of giant cannibals, ruled over by their king, Antiphates, and his queen.

Odysseus sent a few of his men to scout out the land. While looking for food and shelter, some of the men were captured and eaten by Antiphates. The rest ran back towards their ships, but the giants threw boulders at the vessels and sank them in the harbor. The only ship left intact and able to escape was Odysseus's.

MYTH AND REALITY
The Ancient Greeks likened the winds to horses, because they moved so swiftly. The Spartans even sacrified a horse to the god of the winds.

CIRCE THE ENCHANTRESS

Odysseus and his few remaining men set sail once again. This time they landed on Aeaea, home to the goddess, Circe, a beautiful enchantress, skilled in magic.

Circe invited the men to a feast, where she gave them food, but also a potion that turned them into pigs! Odysseus, who had stayed with the ship, was enraged by Circe's treachery and set off immediately to her palace to rescue his men.

On the way, he met the messenger god, Hermes (see page 66), who told him to eat a special herb to protect him from Circe's spells. Odysseus took Hermes's advice and was able to overpower Circe and make her change his men back into humans.

Odysseus and Circe fell in love and he remained on Aeaea for a year. Eventually, his men became restless and convinced Odysseus to leave the island and head for home once again. Circe told Odysseus that to get home, he and his crew must visit the Underworld and speak to the spirit of Tiresias, a blind prophet, who would tell them the way.

THE BLIND PROPHET

Odysseus and his men traveled to the river Acheron—the river of pain, and one of the five rivers of the Underworld. They offered up sacrifices to Hades, god of the Underworld, before Odysseus entered the land of the dead.

Odysseus finally met the shade (soul) of the prophet Tiresias, who revealed that Odysseus and his crew were being punished by Poseidon for blinding his son, Cyclops. Tiresias told Odysseus that he would eventually return home, though he would first need to face two monsters, Scylla and Charybdis. He also told Odysseus not to touch the cattle of the Sun in the land of Thrinacia. With these warnings ringing in his ears, Odysseus left Tiresias.

While in the Underworld, Odysseus met other spirits, too. He met the shades of men and heroes—including those he fought with in the Trojan War—and listened to their sad stories. Odysseus was mobbed by souls wanting to know about their living loved ones. Frightened, he ran back to his ship and sailed away.

← – – – – | Odysseus visits Tiresias, the blind prophet, in the Underworld.

MYTH AND REALITY
The Ancient Greeks believed that the Underworld could be reached by following five rivers—Acheron, Styx, Lethe, Cocytus, and Phlegethon.

THE SIRENS

Odysseus returned to Aeaea, where he spent one last night with Circe. She warned him about the Sirens—beautiful birdlike creatures who lured sailors to their deaths with their enchanting song.

A few days after Odysseus and his crew left Aeaea, they came close to the Sirens.

Following Circe's advice, he plugged the ears of his men with wax, so they could not hear the sound. But Odysseus wanted to know what their beautiful song sounded like. He had his men tie him to the ship's mast and ordered them not to release him, no matter how much he begged. Odysseus was only untied when the Sirens were safely out of earshot.

The Sirens singing to Odysseus and his men.

MYTH AND REALITY
The phrase "between Scylla and Charybdis" has entered the English language. It has come to mean being faced by two great dangers.

Scylla and Charybdis on either side of the treacherous sea.

SCYLLA AND CHARYBDIS

Odysseus and his crew then had to face the twin dangers of Scylla and Charybdis, which had been predicted by the prophet Tiresias. Scylla was a terrifying six-headed monster that wanted to eat six men from each passing ship to satisfy its hunger; Charybdis was a huge and violent whirlpool in the sea, able to swallow entire ships. Navigating the waters between Scylla and Charybdis was no easy feat. Odysseus steered his ships close to the cliffs, while his men kept a watchful eye on Charybdis on the other side of the strait. But as their attention was distracted, Scylla swallowed six of Odysseus's crewmen.

LAST MAN STANDING

Next, Odysseus and his men arrived at Thrinacia, which was the island of the Sun god, Helios. Odysseus wanted to press on, but his crew convinced him to stop in order to rest and get more supplies.

A violent storm arose, and the men were stuck on the island for a month. Remembering the prophecy of Tiresias, Odysseus forbade his men to kill and eat any of the cattle of the Sun that roamed on the island. At first, the crew survived by eating the food they had on their ship; but soon, they became hungry. While Odysseus slept, the men slaughtered the cattle and began to feast.

Helios soon discovered what the men had done, and asked Zeus to punish Odysseus and his men. So as the men set sail once again, Zeus summoned up another powerful storm, which destroyed the ship and sent all the men to the bottom of the sea. Only heroic Odysseus escaped death by clinging to the wreckage of his ship.

MYTH AND REALITY

Odysseus's journey home took ten years. He would have visited modern-day Spain, Libya, Sardinia, Italy, Greece, and many islands in the Mediterranean.

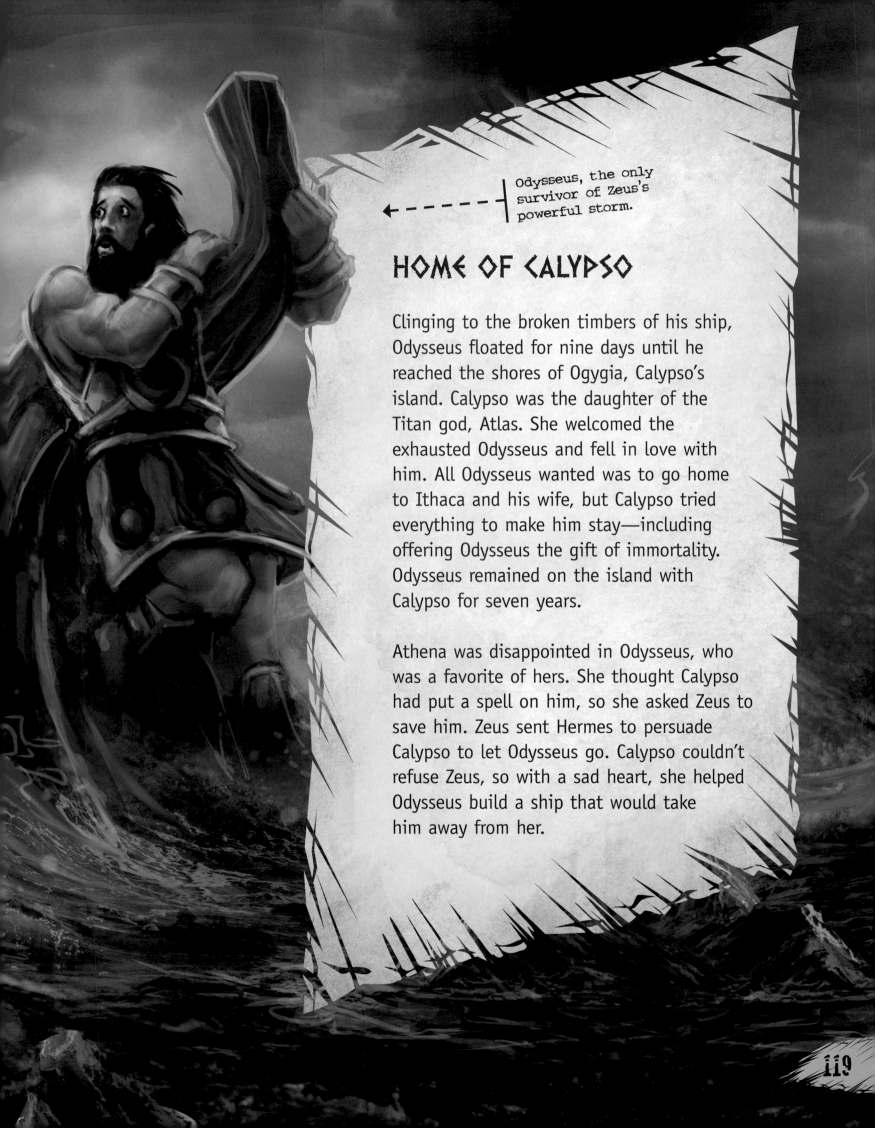

Odysseus, the only survivor of Zeus's powerful storm.

HOME OF CALYPSO

Clinging to the broken timbers of his ship, Odysseus floated for nine days until he reached the shores of Ogygia, Calypso's island. Calypso was the daughter of the Titan god, Atlas. She welcomed the exhausted Odysseus and fell in love with him. All Odysseus wanted was to go home to Ithaca and his wife, but Calypso tried everything to make him stay—including offering Odysseus the gift of immortality. Odysseus remained on the island with Calypso for seven years.

Athena was disappointed in Odysseus, who was a favorite of hers. She thought Calypso had put a spell on him, so she asked Zeus to save him. Zeus sent Hermes to persuade Calypso to let Odysseus go. Calypso couldn't refuse Zeus, so with a sad heart, she helped Odysseus build a ship that would take him away from her.

Odysseus, in disguise, tries to impress Penelope.

MYTH AND REALITY
The home of Odysseus was the island of Ithaca, off the west coast of Greece. It was an important island in ancient times, but today only about 1,000 people live there.

THE BEST SHIP

Odysseus sailed away from a heartbroken Calypso in his new ship. But very soon, another violent storm blew him off course. Bedraggled, exhausted, and unrecognizable, he washed ashore on the land of the Phaeacians. Here, princess Nafsica found Odysseus lying on the beach and took him to the palace of her parents—the king and queen. They welcomed him and had their musicians play songs about the Trojan War.

Being reminded of the war and of his dead friends by this beautiful music made Odysseus very sad. The king and queen asked him why he was overcome by grief. He revealed his true identity to them and told of all the struggles he'd had in trying to reach his home.

The Phaeacians were so honored to have such a famous hero in their midst that they gave Odysseus their fastest ship, plenty of provisions, and the best crew to help get him home safely. Once again, Odysseus set sail for Ithaca.

THE HOMECOMING

Odysseus finally arrived home in Ithaca. Not knowing what had happened in his long absence, he disguised himself as a beggar to meet his old servants and his son. They told him about the many suitors who had been pursuing his wife, Penelope, while he was away.

Still in disguise, he met Penelope and told her about the bravery of Odysseus in the Trojan War. This moved her so much that she gave her suitors a challenge. Whichever of them could string Odysseus's bow and shoot through twelve axe handles would have her hand in marriage. Each suitor tried and failed. Then, Odysseus, still dressed as a beggar, strung the bow with ease and shot an arrow through all twelve axe handles.

Odysseus then revealed his identity to Penelope, and killed the other suitors. Penelope welcomed her husband and they lived together happily in Ithaca, where Odysseus became a respected and just ruler.

BELLEROPHON AND PEGASUS

Bellerophon was the son of Eurynome, goddess of the meadows, and Poseidon, god of the sea. With gods for parents, he was no ordinary mortal. One day, Bellerophon angered Proteus, a king of Argos. Proteus sent Bellerophon away to his relative, King Iobates, with instructions to have Bellerophon killed. But Iobates liked Bellerophon and couldn't bear to kill him. Instead, he sent him on a near-impossible task—to destroy the Chimera.

Bellerophon riding Pegasus and about to attack the Chimera.

The Chimera was a vicious fire-breathing beast that was part lion, part serpent, and part goat. It had been terrorizing the people who lived nearby.

A prophet told Bellerophon that he would need to catch and tame the winged horse Pegasus to stand any chance of defeating the Chimera. With the help of the goddess Athena, who gave him a magical bridle, Bellerophon was able to mount Pegasus and flew on his back to the lair of the Chimera.

As the monster spewed its fiery breath at Bellerophon, Pegasus flew just out of range of danger, keeping Bellerophon safe. Bellerophon, who was an expert archer, shot many arrows at the beast and killed it.

Bellerophon and Pegasus had many adventures and Bellerophon began to think that he too deserved to be a god. He rode Pegasus up Mount Olympus, but Zeus punished him for his arrogance by knocking him off his horse and back to Earth, where he spent the rest of his days.

MYTH AND REALITY
The name "Chimera" has been taken up by modern science. It is used for an animal or plant that has been genetically changed.

ORPHEUS AND EURYDICE

Orpheus was married to the nymph Eurydice, and he loved her dearly. One day Eurydice was walking through a meadow and was bitten by a poisonous snake. Tragically, she died. Orpheus was so heartbroken that he journeyed to the Underworld to try to get her back. He played his lyre so beautifully there that the shades (souls) forgot their agony and tortures, and he won many hearts. Even Hades, the god of the dead (see page 21), was moved to tears by Orpheus's music.

Hades was so grateful that he granted Orpheus his wish. He could take Eurydice back to Earth, but under one condition: he must lead her out of the Underworld without looking back at her until they reached the surface.

As they were about to emerge into the light of this world, Orpheus forgot Hades's rule and looked back at his wife. She immediately turned into a ghost and vanished. Orpheus was never allowed to enter the Underworld again, so he wandered the Earth forever, crying for his lost love, Eurydice.

Orpheus looks back at Eurydice ⊦ - - - - →

MYTH AND REALITY
A lyre is an ancient string instrument that looks like a small harp. It often had four or seven strings that were plucked to make a sound.

ORPHEUS

- Orpheus was the son of Apollo and Calliope, the muse of poets.

- He was blessed with the gift of music and could even charm trees and rocks when he played his lyre.

- He accompanied Jason in the search for the Golden Fleece (see page 89).

DAEDALUS AND ICARUS

Daedalus was a gifted craftsman who designed beautiful palaces and incredible machines. His statues were so lifelike that they had to be chained up in case they came to life. He was best known for building the Labyrinth—the complicated maze that held the Minotaur, a creature that was half man, half bull (see page 86). The labyrinth was beneath the palace of King Minos on the island of Crete.

Minos did not want anyone to know the secrets of the labyrinth, so he imprisoned its designer, Daedalus, and his son, Icarus, in a tower. However, Daedalus was too clever for the king. He invented an ingenious way to escape.

Deadalus collected feathers from birds nesting in the tower and glued them together with wax to make wings. Wearing these wings, Daedalus and Icarus managed to fly away from the tower. Daedalus warned Icarus not to fly too close to the Sun, where the heat could melt the wax in the wings, or too close to the sea, where the sea spray could weigh down the feathers.

However, Icarus didn't listen to his father's warnings. He was so excited to be able to fly that he flew too close to the Sun. The wax melted and the wings fell apart. Icarus fell into the sea and drowned.

MYTH AND REALITY
The name of king Minos was given by archaeologists to a real civilization that existed on the island of Crete long before the Greeks. They were called Minoans.

126

Icarus flies too close to the sun.

DAEDALUS

- Daedalus grew up and worked in Athens.

- Daedalus took on his nephew, Talos, as his pupil. He became jealous of Talos's skill and murdered him before fleeing to the court of Minos in Crete.

- After the death of his son, Icarus, Daedalus lived his last years in Sicily.

ATALANTA

- Atalanta was the daughter of Iasus, a prince of Arcadia.

- Her father wanted a son, not a daughter, so he left the infant Atalanta high on a mountainside to die.

- Atalanta was raised by a bear and became a great huntress.

MYTH AND REALITY

Running contests were popular in Ancient Greece. Many people came to watch races of different lengths, or with runners wearing armor or carrying torches.

ATALANTA AND THE FOOT RACE

There once lived a huntress named Atalanta. When she was young, a prophet told her that if she ever married she and her husband would live unhappy lives. So Atalanta was determined to remain unmarried forever.

Atalanta was very beautiful and so had many suitors. For fun, she made them race against her; if they lost the race, they would be put to death. She was so fast that many men died chasing her. A young man named Hippomenes fell in love with Atalanta. He knew that he would lose in a race against her, so appealed to the goddess of love, Aphrodite, for help. The goddess gave him three golden apples and told Hippomenes what to do to win.

During the race Hippomenes dropped one apple at a time. Atalanta stopped each time to pick up the apple, and so Hippomenes overtook her and won the race. Foolishly, the young man forgot to thank Aphrodite for her help, which angered the goddess.

As a punishment, Aphrodite turned both Atalanta and Hippomenes into leopards, and many people believe that the two still race each other to this day.

← - - - - - - - Hippomenes overtakes Atalanta by dropping golden apples.

THE LABORS OF HERACLES

Zeus's wife, Hera, hated Heracles from birth because he was Zeus's son by Alcmena. She sent two snakes to kill him when he was just an infant, but Heracles strangled them. As he grew, Hera hated him even more. She struck him with a fit of madness, which made Heracles kill his own wife, Megara, and their sons. Heracles asked the Oracle of Delphi how he could make up for his mad actions. The Oracle told him to go to Tiryns and obey the orders of its king, Eurystheus. The king set Hercules ten tasks, or labors, which—when completed—would give him a place among the gods.

THE NEMEAN LION

The first task that Heracles had to accomplish was to kill the fearsome Nemean lion. This wild beast roamed the plains around Tiryns, terrifying the inhabitants. Heracles first tried to shoot the lion with magic arrows, which he had been given by the god Apollo. The lion had such tough skin that the arrows could not pierce it. So Heracles fought and killed the beast with his bare hands. He took its impenetrable skin as a trophy and wore it as armor from that day on.

HERACLES

- Heracles was the son of Zeus and Alcmena, the wife of Amphitryon, king of Tiryns.
- He was considered to be the strongest and bravest of all mortals.
- He was renowned for his skill with a bow and arrow, and for his wrestling.

MYTH AND REALITY

According to legend, Zeus put the lion killed by Heracles into the sky as the constellation Leo, which resembles a crouching lion.

Heracles struggles to
kill the Nemean lion
with his bow and arrow.

THE HYDRA

The second task that King Eurystheus set for Heracles was to kill the Hydra, a nine-headed serpent that was sacred to Hera. This fearsome creature could spit poisonous venom at its enemies.

Heracles, accompanied by his brave nephew Iolaus, drove his chariot to the Hydra's den. Heracles lured the monster out and began to beat it with his club. But as soon as he smashed one of the Hydra's heads, two more grew in its place. Heracles called for his nephew's help. As soon as Heracles cut off one of the heads, his nephew would burn the stump with a torch; this prevented the heads from growing back.

Even though Heracles had completed the task, the king did not acknowledge his success, because Heracles had been helped by his nephew.

MYTH AND REALITY
The hydra gave its name to a small tentacled animal that lives in fresh water. Hydras are strange because they never seem to age.

The golden hind with Artemis and Apollo, as Heracles tries to capture it.

THE GOLDEN HIND

Heracles's third labor was to find and catch the Ceryneian hind. This was a golden-horned deer that was sacred to Artemis, the goddess of the hunt. It was said to be so swift that it could outrun a flying arrow.

Heracles searched for the creature for a year and finally found it in Arcadia. When he was about to catch the animal, Artemis and her brother Apollo appeared to Heracles. He begged forgiveness from Artemis, and explained that he wished the hind no harm, but had to capture it as one of his labors. The goddess allowed him to take the hind on the condition that he released it as soon as he could. When Heracles returned to Eurystheus, the hind ran all the way back to its mistress, Artemis.

THE ERYMANTHIAN BOAR

Next, King Eurystheus told Heracles to capture and return the Erymanthian boar—a huge, angry wild pig that was terrorizing people and destroying villages around its home on the mountain called Erymanthus.

Heracles found the boar's lair and stood outside, shouting to attract its attention. Soon the boar ran out and brave Heracles ran straight at it. The startled boar ran away and got stuck in a deep snowdrift. Heracles was able to chain up the animal and haul it back to Eurystheus. The king was terrified of the boar, and hid in a pot in terror. He ordered Heracles to throw the boar into the sea.

← – – – – – | King Eurystheus hides in a pot, terrified of the boar he ordered Heracles to catch.

THE FILTHY STABLES

Heracles's fifth labor was a dirty one, designed to humiliate the hero. In one day, he was to clean out the stables where King Augeas kept his animals. This task was thought to be almost impossible because Augeas owned hundreds of animals, and the stables had not been cleaned in 30 years.

Heracles accomplished this task in an ingenious way. He dug two deep trenches all the way from the stables to two rivers that flowed nearby. He then diverted water from the rivers along the ditches so that it gushed through the stables, carrying away all the mess.

However, Eurystheus refused to count Heracles's success in this labor because he claimed that the rivers—rather than Heracles—had done all the work.

KING EURYSTHEUS

- Eurystheus was the cousin of Heracles and the grandson of Perseus (see page 94).
- He was the king of Tiryns—a kingdom that should rightly have belonged to Heracles.
- Eurystheus remained a bitter enemy of Heracles until his death.

MAN-EATING BIRDS

Hercules's sixth labor was to drive away a flock of vicious, man-eating birds that terrorized the Arcadian forests near the town of Stymphalos. These birds had long legs, metal-tipped wings, and razor-sharp claws. They could not be approached easily because they lived on a sticky bog.

Heracles first scared the birds by shaking a giant bronze rattle made by Hephaestus, the god of blacksmiths (see page 46). As the startled birds rose into the air above their swampy home, Heracles shot them down with arrows tipped with the poisonous blood of the Hydra, which he had slain in his second labor.

THE CRETAN BULL

Heracles traveled to the island of Crete to complete the next labor set by Eurystheus. This was to capture the beautiful bull that the sea god Poseidon had given to Minos, the king of Crete. The bull had caused much damage in Crete by uprooting trees and crops, and

so Minos was happy to be rid of it. Heracles wrestled with the beast, eventually subdued it, and brought it back to Eurystheus. The bull was released unharmed to wander around the city of Marathon.

THE MARES OF DIOMEDES

For his eighth labor, Heracles was ordered to tame and capture four wild and savage horses that belonged to Diomedes, the king of Thrace. Diomedes was a vicious ruler, who kept his horses mean by feeding them human flesh.

Heracles sailed to Thrace with a band of helpers. He overpowered the stable hands and freed the horses from their heavy chains. He drove the horses to the sea but was pursued by Diomedes and his men. Heracles fought and killed Diomedes, and fed his body to the horses. After feeding on their evil master's body, the horses became tame, and Heracles was able to take them back to Eurystheus.

Heracles fires a poisoned arrow at a man-eating bird. ├ - - - - →

HIPPOLYTA

- Hippolyta was queen of the Amazons, and daughter of the war god Ares.
- The Amazons would kill their male children or send them away into the wilderness.
- Hippolyta led the Amazons in many battles against the Greeks.

Heracles meeting Hippolyta, queen of the Amazons.

138

THE BELT OF HIPPOLYTA

For his ninth labor, Heracles traveled to the land of the Amazons—a fierce, warlike race of women. His task was to fetch the belt owned by Hippolyta, queen of the Amazons. This was a special belt that gave its owner great power.

At first, Hippolyta was awestruck by Heracles and was willing to give him the belt. But then Hera appeared disguised as an Amazon, and spread false rumors that Heracles had really come to kidnap Hippolyta. The Amazons thought their queen was under threat and attacked Heracles and his men, who made a hasty retreat, with Hippolyta's belt as a prize.

MYTH AND REALITY
The Amazons may have really existed. Archaeologists have found ancient graves of tall female warriors in the country of Kazakhstan.

CATTLE OF GERYON

Heracles's next task was to bring back the cattle that belonged to the monstrous creature Geryon, who had three heads, six hands, and three bodies joined at the waist. For this task, Heracles had to sail beyond the Mediterranean and into the Atlantic Ocean. Legend has it that his path was blocked by a range of mountains that joined Africa to Europe. Heracles split the mountains with a blow of his club, making a passage flanked by great cliffs, called the pillars of Heracles.

When Heracles found the cattle, he first had to kill their two-headed watchdog, Orthus. Next he killed Eurytion, a son of Ares, the war god, who guarded the cattle, and then Geryon himself.

As he drove the cattle back to Tiryns, he ran into further obstacles, including the monster Cacus who stole eight cows. When they finally arrived at Tiryns, Eurystheus sacrificed the cattle to Hera.

When Heracles had completed the ten tasks, Eurystheus did not accept that he had completed them all single-handed. In conquering the Hydra he had been helped by his nephew, and in cleaning the Augean Stables, he had used the power of two mighty rivers. So Eurystheus set Heracles two additional tasks.

APPLES OF THE HESPERIDES

The eleventh labor was to fetch the golden apples that the goddess Gaea had given to Hera on her wedding day. The apples were guarded by maidens called the Hesperides. They were the daughters of Atlas—the Titan who held the world on his shoulders (see page 14).

Heracles convinced Atlas to get the apples for him. While Atlas was away, Heracles promised to bear the world on his own shoulders. Atlas was glad to be rid of the burden and gladly agreed to help. When he returned with the apples, Atlas didn't want to return to his old job. Heracles said he'd continue to hold the world, but asked if Atlas could hold it just for a moment while he got more comfortable. As Atlas did so, Heracles quickly ran away with the apples.

CERBERUS

Heracles's final labor was to capture Cerberus, the three-headed dog that guarded the gates of the Underworld— the realm of the dead. With help from the gods Athena, Hermes, and Hestia, Heracles crossed the river Styx, which was the boundary between Earth and the Underworld. Heracles found Hades, the god of the Underworld, and asked if he could take Cerberus back to the world of the living. Hades agreed, but on one condition—Heracles had to overcome the giant dog without using any weapons.

Heracles wrestled the dog barehanded, subdued it, and carried it out of the Underworld. When he brought it to Eurystheus, the king was terrified and made Heracles return Cerberus to the Underworld.

On completing his labors, Heracles was rewarded by his father Zeus with the gift of immortality and eternal youth. He married Hebe, the daughter of Zeus and Hera, much to the annoyance of Hera, who continued to dislike Heracles.

Heracles attempting to catch Cerberus

MYTH AND REALITY
Dogs were valued by the Ancient Greeks for hunting and guarding animals. Dogs were also kept as pets and sometimes buried with their owners.

GLOSSARY

anvil
A heavy block of iron with a flat top and rounded sides, used by a blacksmith to shape pieces of metal.

apostle
One of the 12 special followers of Jesus Christ.

Asphodel Fields
The place in the Underworld where the souls of ordinary mortals went after death.

boar
A wild pig, often large and covered with hair.

bridle
A head harness used to lead and control a horse.

Celts
A group of people who lived in Europe long before the Roman Empire.

centaur
A mythological creature said to be half-horse and half-human.

Chaos
The state of disorganization that existed before the start of time.

constellation
A group of stars that makes a pattern in the night sky.

Cyclopes
A race of mythological giants who had a single large eye in the forehead.

dryad
In Greek myth, a female spirit of a tree.

Elysian/Elysium
The paradise to which the souls of heroes went after their death.

Fates
Also called the Moirai, the three sister goddesses who controlled the destinies of mortals on Earth.

festival
A regular celebration held by the Ancient Greeks to honor a god or goddess. Festivals often included athletics, art, feasting, and drinking.

forge
A furnace where metal is heated so it can be shaped by a blacksmith.

Giants
A mythological race of people of huge strength, born from the spilt blood of Uranus.

Harpy
A voracious monster with the head of a woman and body of a bird.

hearth
A fireplace—the focal point of home for the Ancient Greeks.

Hecatoncheires
Hundred-armed mythological giants with great destructive powers, who lived in Tartarus.

ivory
The hard bonelike material that makes up an elephant's tusks.

labyrinth
A deliberately confusing path or maze.

Muse
One of nine Greek goddesses, each of whom inspired artists, scientists, or other thinkers.

Nymph
A goddess in Greek mythology. Nymphs were usually associated with one aspect of nature, such as rivers, trees, or flowers.

Olympian
One of the 12 main gods of Ancient Greece all of whom, except Hades, lived on Mount Olympus.

Oracle
A priest or priestess who was able to communicate with the gods or give advice about the future.

pomegranate
A fruit that contains hundreds of fleshy red seeds. These fruits were very popular in Ancient Greece.

Primordials
The very first beings to come into existence, according to Greek myth.

sacrifice
An offering to appease a god or goddess. Animals were often sacrificed to the Greek gods.

satyr
A forest god with a human face and body, but the legs and tail of a horse.

sickle
A semicircular metal blade, usually used for cutting grasses or crops.

Syrinx
A wind instrument made from a set of hollow reeds tied together. Sometimes also called Pan pipes.

Tartarus
The lowest and darkest reaches of the Underworld where the Titans were imprisoned after their defeat by the Olympian gods. The place reserved for the most wicked souls after death.

Titan
Gods of huge strength who were descended from the primordials and who came before the Olympian gods.

Underworld
The place where souls went after death.

INDEX